Cities of Lonesome Fear

GORDON MCLEAN

MOODY PRESS
CHICAGO

ISBN: 0-8024-1136-3

3 5 7 9 10 8 6 4

Printed in the United States of America

In the streets they cry out . . .
all joy turns to gloom, all gaiety is banished

Isaiah 24:11

To
Arthur and Gladys DeKruyter,
Dick and Mary Norton,
partners in sharing God's love
and answering the cry

Dave and Neta Jackson have written more than thirty books on their own, including books for children, Bible studies, historical fiction, and books on church life, relationships, marriage, and family. They have also authored twenty books with other people. Dave and Neta are members of Reba Place Church in Evanston, Illinois, where they have been involved in pastoral and other church ministry since 1973. The Jacksons have two children, Julian and Rachel.

Other books by Gordon McLean:

Coming in on the Beam: A Look At America's Teenagers
We're Holding Your Son
High on the Campus (with Haskell Bowen)
Hell Bent Kid
God Help Me, I'm a Parent
Where the Love Is
Man, I Need Help
The Care and Feeding of Parents
How to Raise Your Parents
Let God Manage Your Money
Christians and Crime
Terror in the Streets
Danger at Your Door

Contents

Foreword

When I was a teenager growing up in Baltimore in the '60s, gangs were a way of life. However, the meaning, nature, purpose, and pathology of gangs then differed greatly from their nature and ethos today. While there has always been a violent remnant of youth in every city, what normatively typified gang activity in those days was littering, breaking windows, playing hooky from school to go with a group to a movie, or just hanging out on the corner trying to harmonize after the likes of The Temptations, Miracles, or The Delfonics.

Today, however, the word *gang* has a whole new level of meaning. It stands for violence, drugs, sexual assaults, harassment, social deterioration, anarchy, police crackdowns, massive prison populations, and new prison construction. Urban gangs have become the dominant urban threat. Of all the factors underscoring the new American image of gangs stands one overriding reality, namely, *gangs today represent a replacement of the family rather than merely an extension of the family.*

This new family tie means that gangs set their own standards, values, perspectives, rules, and code of ethics. And as in any family, these guidelines are passed on to other family members both by precept and example. This fact alone makes gangs a most challenging reality to confront.

Gordon McLean gives an excellent analysis and critique of the reality of contemporary gang life. But he does so not from an isolated academic perspective but from a gut level, heart wrenching personal one. He knows of what he speaks because he has been there, lived there, worked there, suffered there, and served there. *Cities of Lonesome Fear* brings you inside the gang family and lets you talk with its members. It allows you to unmask the kids behind the statistics and think as they think, feel as they feel, suffer as they suffer, and survive as they survive.

If, though, this were all that Gordon's work accomplished, it would have missed the mark. On the contrary, it hits a bull's eye because it goes beyond a mere description of the gang reality to demonstrate what the power of God can do in transforming the minds of gang members because of the regenerating work of Jesus Christ. This book takes Christ out of the comfortable pews and off the stained glass windows and unleashes Him behind prison walls, into poverty impoverished, violence infested neighborhoods and demonstrates clearly what Christians can do when they introduce the gospel of Christ as the only real answer to the crisis of meaninglessness now plaguing our inner city youth.

A significant product of Mr. McLean's work is that all Christians who read it will be challenged to examine their own calling to determine whether they are hiding from God's call on their lives. Maybe, just maybe, God wants you to invest your life in helping to create a new kind of gang, God's gang, where our kids will find hope instead of despair, meaning instead of madness, and purpose instead of mere existence. *Cities of Lonesome Fear* is for every Christian who is serious about making a difference in our country and who is willing to take the risk and say, "Here am I, Lord, send me!"

DR. ANTHONY T. EVANS, TH.D.
Senior Pastor, Oak Cliff Bible Fellowship
President, The Urban Alternative

Introduction

Our names are Tony and Burn. We have a few things we'd like to say about this book.

On the streets of the city we've been enemies. Our boys are at war. We've seen our friends wounded, and some have died. Others of our partners, still in their teens as we are, have been locked up, and they'll be in prison for most of their lives. We've stood by helplessly as mothers, sisters, and girlfriends have cried in hospital emergency rooms and at funerals for kids much too young, or in courtrooms, where more tragedies occurred.

That's what it's like growing up in urban America. We know. We're still here. To us a "quiet street" is scary; it means something is about to happen. We like plenty of lights and noise; then we know things are normal. No matter what we are doing out there, we never really relax. Stop and talk to us and we'll listen, but we'll also watch every car coming down the street. It may have an enemy at the wheel. We'll glance at every passer-by and constantly eye the shadowed gangways between the houses where an armed enemy could suddenly jump out. We live in a battle zone. And often it's the one who shoots first who lives to tell about it later.

We're in two Chicago youth street gangs. One of us (Tony) is a member of the Ambrose, the other (Burn) is a Bishop. The hatred between our groups has been long and deep. The scars and the tombstones are there to remind us of the bitter rivalry and its tragic results.

Yet here we are together, writing an introduction to a book. How can that be?

First, this is more than a book about gangs. The details of street wars you can catch on the evening TV news or in the papers. This is a book about an answer, about hope, and one man's daring to believe that, through God, kids in the toughest neighborhoods can change. This book also says, If God can change us, He can meet the needs of people in your world, in the nice communities, on the campus, at the job.

Second, we write together because the Lord has changed us. I (Tony) joined the Ambrose before I was a teenager. It was a place to find action and excitement. I figured nothing could ever touch me. But I've been shot five times, one a very painful .38 bullet wound in my wrist from a Bishop. Later, I spent nine months in the youth section of the county jail before I was cleared of an attempted murder charge.

It was in jail that I met Gordon McLean and his partners from Youth For Christ who came regularly to tell us about the Lord. I had good training at home, went to a church school, and knew all the right stuff about God. But I had never listened to Him and what He wanted to say to me. Then God put me where I had no choice but to listen and think, and I finally came to know Him.

Since I (Burn) carry shrapnel in my body, I guess you could call me a Chicago vet. I've lost four of my boys to the Ambrose and their allies in the shooting street war that rages between us. Tony's boys have a reputation for violence. One of my best friends, Buff, had just stepped off a bus after his first day on a new job. It was also his birthday. He was one cool guy. Then a car pulled up, right there on a busy street, and two guys with guns jumped out and blasted away. Buff never knew what hit him. Three Ambrose were charged with the murder.

Five months earlier I was shot in the chest by the Ambrose; the bullet partially paralyzed my left arm. It was a drive-by shooting like the gangs in Los Angeles and Chicago are famous for. I was standing with a group of my boys and was hit. That's how I got the shrapnel. I'm still going through extensive therapy to get the full use of my arm again.

Before joining the Bishops I had become a Deuce at age twelve. I was a "crank," a crazy kid. But I wanted more power and people to back me up, as well as the chance to make some tall money on the streets, so I switched over to the Bishops. We partied, got high, sold drugs, and pulled hits together. The whole thing seemed pretty exciting at the time—though I didn't like watching our older boys go to jail or my partners get killed.

Gordon McLean and his helpers knew some of our boys at the jail and worked with them when they came home. That's how I met them. Then I was asked to attend a Christian youth conference in Washington, D.C., filling in for Ralphie, one of my friends who couldn't go at the last minute because his mother was in the hospital.

Suddenly I was traveling across the country with guys from rival gangs, even staying in the same hotel and finally in the same room with guys I'd met only at the business end of a loaded gun. We got along well, even became friends, which amazed all of us. We wanted the same things in life: a family, a job, and a happy, worthwhile life. The excitement of eight thousand Christian kids was contagious, and I opened my life to the Lord. It was a real change.

But I came home to a tragedy. Ralphie, the boy whose place I took, had been gunned down and killed in the street while I was on the trip. Right now I'm trying to help our young guys—"shortys" we call them—get their lives on the right track. It isn't always easy, but I'm not giving up. I've been through police stations, the courts, jail, hospital emergency rooms, street fights, shootings, stabbings, and ended up—with the Lord. And with Him is the only place to be. That's where I'm coming from.

Together we (Burn and Tony) went to another Christian youth conference in Indianapolis and got to know each other along with some guys from other gangs who were our opposition. Now we're more than friends; we're brothers because we are members of God's family. Of course, several of our boys still don't understand or accept what we're trying to say. But we've got to do what's right and reach out to them whenever we can. And *some* do listen.

God is at work. That's what this is all about. In our world, in yours. Walking with Him has been a rewarding experience for one unique man, Gordon McLean, as you'll find out on these pages. Then maybe you'll be encouraged to take some steps of faith in your own life, even though it may be completely different from where we are.

We want you to share in some miracles. We represent a major miracle ourselves: two former rivals signing this introduction together. But there are more on the pages that follow.

TONY SNELIUS
BURN MENDIA

Part 1

WHY KIDS JOIN GANGS

1

Not My Idea of a Good Time

Up ahead I could see several large buildings outlined dimly by the moon shining through breaks in the clouds and by an occasional street light. I knew just enough about where we were to know that I didn't belong there.

As I drove, Glenn sat beside me giving directions; in the back sat his friend Mookie. Both were African-American young men in their late teens, veterans of the urban jungle with considerable experience in street wars, gang rivalry, and the violent battles for turf power and control of drug trafficking that are facts of life in the inner city.

I met both youths when they were confined at the juvenile detention center in Chicago. They had participated in our counseling groups as part of the chapel program, and we actually became good friends. They told me that when they got out of detention they would show me around their world. In one of my weaker moments I agreed, and tonight was the payoff on the promised tour.

I had not given the idea of going out with them a second thought, but Glenn and Mookie had not forgotten. They were quite determined to educate their white minister friend on life in the ghetto and introduce me to their partners in the Vice Lords organization. The planned trip through the Henry Horner Homes, one of the big Chicago Housing Authority complexes, was not my version of a good idea any time, certainly not late on a foggy fall night.

It was only supposed to be a drive-through of some neighborhood streets. But once we got going the boys' enthusiasm to expand the original trip began to grow. Now we were not only going to the housing project but up to a friend's apartment.

I had no idea when the last white person had been in that complex at night or if he ever came out, but I had absolutely no desire to make history—all of which I expressed to my eager friends. But they were not to be deterred; we were going in, and that was final.

"You have nothing to worry about," Glenn said, trying to sound confident and reassuring. "All the guys in that building know me."

"That's not the issue," I replied, anxious not to sound as nervous as I actually was. "The question is not do they *know* you, but do they *like* you?" The difference between "knowing" and "liking" on the streets is spelled s-u-r-v-i-v-a-l, which, I reminded my friends, was a high priority for me.

Meanwhile, I was praying fervently. "God, what did You get me into now? I might be knocking at the door of Your house a lot sooner than I figured—like tonight."

It was another situation I never imagined a guy like me being involved in. I had been born in Regina and raised in Victoria, two quiet Canadian cities. But after I became a Christian, I soon learned that to sign on with the Lord and move within His will can take a person places he or she never imagined. As an urban missionary, going with God this particular night took me to some of the most dangerous streets in America. I was driving with Glenn and Mookie on the west side of Chicago.

"Here You and I go again, Lord," I muttered, putting special emphasis on "You" as Glenn directed me into the parking lot and we found a place to park. Even my car seemed strangely out of place. I surveyed a wide assortment of multi-colored refugees from junkyards that appeared to have only one thing that worked properly: radios blaring at full volume.

"Let's go," Glenn said impatiently, opening the door and jumping out before I had turned off the ignition. "What are you waiting for?"

"I'm saying good-bye to my car. I may never see it again."

"C'mon, man; you've got nothin' to worry about. I'll tell a couple of the boys to keep an eye on it for you."

"Great. And who's going to watch them?"

"That's the trouble with you, Rev—you don't have no confidence," Glenn said disgustedly, calling me by one of my nicknames among the kids and accurately reading what was going through my mind.

We walked across the dimly lit parking lot past a number of observers who did not hide their amazement to see me with Glenn and Mookie. Then we went into the hallway. There was no door, and the corridors were even gloomier than the parking lot. The few dim bulbs revealed walls scrawled with gang graffiti. It was anybody's guess what the original color had been. At the elevator, a young man stood guard; his job was to collect a dollar per ride—for the gang treasury—from residents wanting to go up to their apartments on any of the ten floors. Glenn nodded at him; the boy smiled back. Our ride was free.

The light in the elevator was out, so Mookie thoughtfully flicked on a cigarette lighter for our ride to the top. We got off at an another dimly lit hallway and proceeded to an apartment door of heavy metal designed to delay any potential raiders—police *or* rivals. Glenn banged loud enough to be heard over the radio blaring at full volume inside and announced our arrival. The door opened, and we stepped in.

What light there was inside came from two small green and red bulbs on opposite sides of the room. I made out some dim figures moving about or sitting down. After my eyes adjusted, I counted four young men and two young women smoking and drinking beer.

Glenn pointed to a vacant spot on the couch and told me to sit down. Mookie joined me while Glenn got into an intense conversation with several of the boys.

"They think you must be a cop," Mookie whispered to me. "Ain't nobody else makes unscheduled house calls around here. But pretty soon they'll figure that since you came in with us, you ain't the heat bringin' trouble."

"How soon?" I asked nervously.

Mookie smiled, ignored my question, and noted, "Then they'll want to know if you're sellin', buyin', or usin'—if you ain't no cop. But don't worry, Glenn'll tell 'em you just visitin'."

Soon the group broke up and came over. Glenn introduced me as his preacher friend. "Preacher" was nice; "friend" was what counted. The guys all wore dark glasses. Each gave me his street name and shook hands.

Glenn then went into the other room with the boys and left me to talk with one of the girls sitting by me on the couch.

"You really a preacher?" she asked, more curious than hostile. "I ain't never talked to one, you know, face-to-face." She paused, then continued. "I'm Linai. That's my baby over there."

In the far corner of the room I could barely make out a crib with an infant in it. Linai went over, picked up the baby, and held her while we talked.

The little girl was six months old, and Linai seemed very devoted to her. "I don't know where her father is," she volunteered. I nodded, thinking that being a single parent has to be one of the toughest jobs in the world and in that environment doubly hard if not impossible.

Linai seemed to want to talk. "At first, when I was expecting, my mother wanted me to get rid of the kid and so did my o' man [the baby's father, Linai's boyfriend]. You know, he wanted me to have an abortion. But that didn't seem right to me; I wanted my baby. When he couldn't persuade me to change my mind, my o' man just disappeared, and I ain't seen him since. Now I just want to be a good mother."

"Do you have an apartment of your own?" I asked.

"This is my place now. The boys here take care of me. I don't want my little girl growing up here, but—well, right now I don't have no other choice. Maybe someday I can get a job and get another place, and it will be better."

Before I could comment the boys came back in, turned down the radio, and came over to the couch.

"So you're a friend of Glenn and Mookie," the more talkative youth said. He shook his head. "Those guys are always comin' up with something crazy. But bringing you here . . ." He just shook his head again. They all laughed.

"Tell me, white boy, aren't you scared?"

I hate it when they call me "boy," but I let it pass. "Should I be?" I asked.

"Not really. You're a friend of theirs. We'll give you respect." He paused for a moment, then broke the silence to suddenly ask, "Are you heavy into the Bible stuff?"

Well, here goes, I thought. "Yes, I am. It's the best thing any of us have going."

"How do you figure?"

"It's got sixty-six books in it that our Father wrote, and it tells us how we can know Him and get some good things happening in our lives. Without it, well, life's just kind of a blank page . . ."

"With a lot of mad scribbles, right?" another boy volunteered.

"You really believe God cares about us?" a third boy asked cynically. "Look, you know what we do here. We got to survive. There ain't no jobs around, the schools don't want us, so we sell—you know, deal drugs. Glenn brought you to a *spot*, a cocaine house. How do you and your Jesus like that?"

"I despise it," I replied firmly. "And He does, too. Yet God looks beyond what we do because He knows what we are—often lonely, searching, scared people, doing things we know are wrong because we're so empty inside. You make your money off people's misery and then hate yourself for it. But God can change all that."

"Well, we don't hate the *money* when we've got it," one boy said with a laugh.

"Dealing is just a way to earn a buck," another spoke up.

"What do you really believe about doing drug sales for a living?" I asked. "Would you want your little brothers doing it?"

"My little brother is a runner now, and he's only nine," one guy volunteered.

"I didn't ask you if he did it. I asked if that's what you *want* him doing?"

"No, not really," he admitted. "But you don't understand what we're about. You're white, drive a nice car, live in a good neighborhood, get a regular paycheck. You've never had to live on the streets."

"You're right." It was my turn to admit it. It *was* a different world. "But I work for someone who knows all there is to know about suffering and rejection."

They were listening, so I kept going. "When Jesus was born, the only place available was a barn. The king wanted to kill Him, so His family had to skip town to save their child. Later, as He walked the streets telling people how to know God, crowds would cheer Him one day and plot how to kill Him the next. One of His own boys sold Him out. If He had a P.D.,[1] the guy was no good; the judge was on the take and listening to the politicians. The jury was rigged against Him, but it didn't matter because the state's[2] already had a fix in."

"Sounds like Chicago, don't it?" Glenn suggested to general laughter.

"Worse," I added. "He got the death sentence, and for nothing. Even that wasn't quick like an injection or the chair but crucifixion on a cross. And finally He was buried in a borrowed grave. Now do you want to tell me He had it easy or doesn't understand people who suffer?" I asked, concluding my impromptu sermon.

"For once a white man got the worst deal," one of the guys said.

"You're wrong," I responded. "Forget all those paintings of a weak, blue-eyed, light-skinned Jesus you see around. His mother and people were Jewish, and He was born in a part of the world where three large continents come together. A white Anglo He was not. He spent His life in the out-of-doors. He worked with His hands as a carpenter. His close friends were fishermen and farmers. He was strong, rugged, and knew His way around deserts and mountains. But He knew His real business—His Father's business—and He never turned from it, even though He knew it would get Him in trouble. He was never selfish or proud. He never set out to hurt someone. And He wants us to know Him so He can help us live that way."

"Huh, not bad," said one of the boys. "Maybe there's more to this Jesus stuff than I thought." He turned to Glenn. "Bring this guy around again. We'll do some more talking."

1. Public defender; a free lawyer.
2. State's attorney; prosecutor.

I wasn't that eager to repeat my visit. Later, when I was again visiting Glenn on the city's west side, one of his buddies asked, "Do you get nervous when you come into our neighborhoods?"

"You might say that." An understatement.

"Let me tell you something," he said. "You're welcome around here. What I want to know is, are *we* welcome in *your* neighborhoods?"

Good question. It made me think. I didn't like the answer we both knew to be true.

But for now our visit was over. I got up, shook hands all around, and we left. The ride down to the main floor was uneventful; my car was still in the parking lot in one piece. With an inner sigh of relief, I drove away with Mookie and Glenn.

It was an evening I would not soon forget.

I'm not the kind of a person who seeks thrills by visiting a dingy cocaine house and talking with young dope dealers. I'm much more comfortable with my suburban friends at church or the Rotary Club—no doubt about it. I would never *choose* to be in that housing project spending time with members of the Vice Lords organization.

But I suspect Jesus would.

It's because of Jesus—and only because of Him—that my staff and I go into the juvenile detention center and the county jail and, yes, even some of the ugly, depressing, dangerous "projects" to talk to kids like Glenn and Mookie and their friends. Because, in spite of everything, in spite of the gangs and violence and drugs and hopelessness, Jesus is making a difference in kids' lives.

BABY BANDITO TAKES A DARE

I have a little shadow,
He follows me in the dark;
If he doesn't mug me on the bus,
He'll get me in the park.

Welcome to Humboldt Park, one of the most gang-infested areas not only in Chicago but in the whole nation. In this predominately Puerto Rican neighborhood, twenty-two rival gangs vie for control, ego, and drug-trafficking rights. The park itself is like the eye of a storm around which swirls the violence and chaos generated by fiery-tempered young Latinos eager to build a "rep" for themselves, largely by doing-in rivals of their own race.

The area is home to Joey, known as "Baby Bandito" on the streets. He joined the Insane Dragons at age eleven. His older brother, Lucan, was shot and killed by a rival, and another infamous Bandito brother, Rubin, became an often-feared gang leader.

Joey was born in New York City. When he was eight the family moved to Chicago to get away from the troubled streets of Brooklyn. They arrived in Humboldt Park long before violence reached the epidemic proportions that now capture national media attention. For Joey, quick to make friends and eager for adventure, the new neighborhood was an exciting world to conquer. He was not going to be an empty suit[3]; he was a Bandito.

I met Joey in the juvenile detention center—"juvie" the kids call it—after one of his many arrests for robbery, drug possession, dealing, you name it. He came to one of our Bible studies and kept coming back. Over time he filled me in on life in the streets.

"You quickly learn the rules of the streets," Joey told me. "Getting caught is only the second worst mistake you can make. First is tricking on a partner to the cops. You don't do that."

Joey got started in the Dragons after being threatened and attacked by rivals who did not like his older brother. Like many younger kids, Joey was eager to impress the gang leaders. He was always ready to lend a helping fist or an extra finger on a trigger. The older boys liked him.

"They paid me to steal things for them. It seemed great. I was having fun and making money, too. Sure, pride in your gang is important. But the main thing is to make bucks. Robbing, burglary, and extortion are ways to do it, but the big, steady money comes in selling drugs." There were plenty of them around: reefer, coke, speed, tic, and of course crack. Chicago

---

3. A nobody.

gang kids kept it out of the area for a while because it undercut the price on more profitable drugs. But now it's a big seller.

As he got older Joey experienced another side to gang life. He saw many of the guys he knew get shot and wounded; more than once he thought it might happen to him. "I was constantly looking back to see if some of the wrong guys might shoot at me. It was a constant battle to control our hood[4] and fight off the enemy."

As he grew up Joey was no stranger to the district police station or to juvenile detention. He was locked up eleven times, but nothing much ever came of the cases.

"Of course not," Joey volunteered. "My partners on the street told any witnesses or victims they better not show up in court. It's amazing how agreeable those people would be when the boys talked to them. It was simply a matter that the cops wouldn't be around all the time and we would. They got the message and did a quick fade on court days."

With such a fast life and apparent sure outcome in court, it was easy for Joey to think he could get away with anything; there was nothing to worry about. "Occasionally a police officer would talk to me and tell me to get out of the gang. But they don't understand. Where I live that's like telling a fish to stay out of water. The gang is our family, our support, our safety, our fun, our money. I wasn't about to quit and couldn't if I wanted too."

But in spite of his brazenness, Joey was not content. Nobody noticed—certainly not his partners in the Dragons, who counted on Joey as a "down member," always game for another night of partying or ready to make a few fast bucks, or the police, to whom he was just another menace to society.

Nora was part of the change. Like his gang partners, Joey could party with a girl one night, then go on to the next one, whether the girl liked it or not. But Nora was not a one-night stand for any guy. She was a loving, caring young lady with something that Joey was short on: a keen sense of values about right and wrong. He liked her from the time they first met, but it was he that would have to adapt to her lifestyle; she had no intention of coming down to his.

4. Neighborhood, turf.

Nora urged Joey to get away from the streets, leave gang wars alone, finish high school, get a job, and plan for the future. "If anyone else talked to me about those things, I turned them off," Joey admitted. "I didn't want to hear that kind of talk. My life was with the boys on the street and all the excitement. Still—I knew she was telling me the truth, and I started listening, even when I didn't want to. I was thinking."

There were some good influences from his early childhood that Joey could not totally shut out, even though he ignored them. Both he and his brother had been Boy Scouts and active in church before they turned to the streets. What he had been taught was still there, dormant but not dead. But what it took to break through to a stubborn, seemingly indifferent young man was another stint in juvenile detention for robbery and extortion.

"I expected to be released after a short stay at the detention center. As usual there would be no victims showing up at court. But then something happened I never expected . . ."

"Something" was an informal Bible study group that I, and several volunteers, hold at the juvenile detention center with guys who want to come out of their unit for counseling. A couple of guys on Joey's unit dared him to go to one of the studies to see if he could stay awake all the way through.

"I actually went to escape the boredom on the unit," Joey admitted. "One night of listening to some talk about the Bible and God couldn't hurt me, I figured, so why not?"

Joey smiles when he thinks back on that session. "If a guy doesn't want to change, that's the worst place in the world to go! I'd be ready if some guy tried to attack me with his fist or a weapon. But I had no defense when those men started talking to me about the Lord.

"Something strange was going on inside me. These guys were telling me I needed to change my whole life. Then when they told me God loved me—that really messed me over! I figured there wasn't much about me or how I lived for God or anyone else to love. That Jesus died on the cross for my sins and wanted to give me a whole new life—well, that blew my mind totally. Nobody I ever knew would do something like that for someone else. We would shine someone on,[5] use each other

5. Mislead them in a con game.

or anyone else. Friendship was more often just partners in misery putting on a cool front. But this news about Jesus was genuine, the real thing."

Several young men prayed that evening to accept Jesus as Lord of their lives, and Joey was one of them.

"I didn't know any good religious words, and I certainly wasn't into praying. But I talked to God that night. I knew I needed to change, and He was the only one who could do it. The Lord and I got together really tight for the first time."

When Joey got back to the unit, the guys were laughing it up, expecting him to tell them what a dumb thing he had just been to. "But," Joey remembers, "you should've seen the look on the face of some of the hard-cores[6] in juvie when one of their homies[7] like me suddenly tells them God has changed his life."

"You gotta be kidding," one startled guy said, instantly serious.

"I'm not kidding at all," Joey replied. "I'm not even sure what happens next. But I've got a *Living Bible* here to read. It's one amazing beginning."

As expected, Joey was soon released. The next to hear about the change in his life were his brother and his partners in the Dragons.

"Rubin was frustrated and angry at first. He figured I wouldn't be a good gang member anymore. Some of the guys thought I'd flipped out. But at that time no one really put me down, especially when they saw I meant it. Some of the guys, especially when no one is around, have asked me seriously about the Lord and what He means to me now."

BABY BANDITO "GROWS UP"

Not only did Joey have to rebuild a set of Christian principles and values, but there was considerable opposition with which to contend. Rival gang members certainly don't believe an enemy changes—they often interpret a change of heart as weakness—so Joey had to be doubly on his guard for a surprise

6. Gang members.
7. Home boys; partners from same neighborhood.

attack. "And the cops don't believe a guy ever changes, either, unless he gets worse," Joey commented.

The school system was also skeptical. Joey was determined to finish high school, even though most of the boys don't. "But if you have a rep on the streets," he told me, "some deans just look for a chance to get rid of you the day you turn sixteen. I had to fight the system to stay in school and had to transfer to another school for my last semester. Most guys just give up and are counted as dropouts when *push*outs is a better word." But Joey would not let the system wear him down; he graduated.

Some boys may face ridicule and minor skirmishes in their own gang when they "cool out," but most kids admire a guy doing things to better himself. There's always an exception, however, and Joey was it.

One of the Dragons—angry over Joey's accomplishments, his willingness to make friends with rivals, and some positive media publicity about a gang member who gave His life to God—was toasted[8] one night and shot Joey three times in the arm and legs. In this instance and with the help of witnesses, the right man was arrested and sentenced to prison. Joey's recovery was slow and painful, but it did not deter him from his new path.

The boy once known as Baby Bandito had to clear some pending cases and serve time, but he looks forward to working at a job instead of dealing drugs, a home and family of his own (even though Nora is no longer in the picture), and spending his spare time working with young kids growing up just as he did on the streets.

Joey's life is merely one example of the power of the gospel to change lives. The "good news" works where nothing else does. And it must happen before other good things (like education and job training) can be effective, because God gives a young person a whole new foundation on which to build his or her life.

Kids like Joey are our responsibility. Christians need to be involved in meeting the spiritual needs of kids who make the

---

8. Burned out on drugs.

headlines. We must go beyond asking, "Why doesn't somebody do something?" when we see the headlines of youth violence. Direct ministry, praying, supporting, and caring do make a difference.

Just as a church wishing to help people victimized in an earthquake sends food and clothing along with Bibles, we must also address the crisis needs of these kids. Christians who are attorneys or police, who serve on juries or work in the justice system, who report in the media, teach school, or are employers all need to see the treatment of these kids as a *Christian* issue. Too often the criminal justice system works to destroy them, not to help them become good citizens. We need to bring biblical principles—a new life, ministry to victims, restitution, fair law enforcement—to solve the crisis.

But one person cannot minister alone; churches need to be involved, especially in reaching out to parents to support them when their kids are in trouble and helping keep their kids away from trouble. And this mission field is in our backyard, right here in the cities and suburbs we call home.

2

The Long Road from Home

For me, working the streets of Chicago as "Rev" to these street gang members was a long way from home.

My parents in Canada had typical dreams and aspirations for their only child, an adopted son. They wanted me to finish school, go to a good college, meet a nice young lady, marry, start a family, and go into either politics or the business world. Pretty straightforward, perfectly acceptable, and certainly not unusual.

But something dramatically altered that plan. As a child in Regina, I often visited the Catholic priests' residence not far from my home. These kindly men gave me, a Protestant boy, a good understanding of the basics of the Christian faith that I was later to treasure much more than I did at the time.

As a high school student, the spiritual seed they had sown began to blossom. I was invited to the Friday evening youth group meetings at the Christian and Missionary Alliance Church. The meetings were fun, and the leaders talked about a relationship with the Lord that went far beyond anything with which I was familiar. On a summer night between my sophomore and junior years I opened my life to the Lord and personally came to know the one who gave His life for me. I did not know what all that meant, but I realized it was a turning point, one that dramatically altered the course of my life.

There was a certain bewilderment in my family at the news of my conversion. My mother had known of the Lord and His Word as a child, but my father said, "You'll get over it," as though it were my first puppy love.

But I did not get over it, and at the end of high school I told my family that I wanted to go into the ministry. That announcement was greeted with even less enthusiasm. While going into the ministry is respectable enough, it does not provide much financial success, and that is where my family and I clashed. Still, I reasoned, we were not *that* far apart. I intended to pastor a nice church on a quiet Canadian street corner and build a career with the appropriate ecclesiastical attainments.

But it turned out that God had quite a different plan for me. When I told Him I would do whatever He wanted, He took me up on it, and I've been busy ever since trying to keep up.

DISCOVERING GOD'S WILL

Finding God's will is not some mystical game of hide-and-seek in which He wants us to agonize over finding the specific spot to which He has called us. God provides two things: open doors and wisdom. Look for the first, ask for the second, and then make intelligent choices. That is discovering His will! If that sounds somewhat dogmatic, then check what the Bible says: "Trust in the Lord with all your heart and lean not on your own understanding; in all your ways acknowledge him, and he will make your paths straight" (Proverbs 3:5-6). My part is to trust and acknowledge, His is to make the path straight. If I am walking with Him, then what I want is what He wants and what He wants is what I want.

Considering my choices, I went to Vancouver, stayed with some friends, and helped in the local Youth For Christ ministry I had joined as a senior in high school. I was planning to enroll in college when another significant detour came along.

Some Christian friends suggested I visit a sixteen-year-old boy being held in jail on a murder charge. I was not interested in the least. I knew nothing about jails except what I had seen on TV (most of which was wrong) and thought I had nothing in common with a killer, even if he was my age.

However, telling some determined Christians you will not do something is not easy. They have a way of using phrases like "spiritual duty," "great opportunity," and "the Lord's will" to move a person in the desired direction. You are especially vulnerable if they sign your paycheck. The prodding worked, though I told them, "I don't think you can get permission for me to go into that jail, but if you can, I will go."

They got the permission, and I went.

My first trip behind bars was unnerving: security checks and heavy, clanging doors that echoed like thunder. Sooner than I realized, I was in a counseling room with a desk and a couple of chairs. A lanky, quiet young man entered, a guard shut the door behind us, and we were alone. My instant reaction was that the officer might have stayed or kept the youth handcuffed or something—I did not want to be alone with a killer, even behind the walls.

"Hi. I'm Gordon McLean."

"I'm Frank." He shook my hand limply as he looked away.

"How you doin'?"

"OK, I guess."

"The food OK in here?"

Frank shrugged.

I sat there.

"You a preacher?"

"No. I mean, I hope to be some day. But I just graduated from high school last June."

"Oh, yeah? What school?"

And then in no time we were talking about our schools, sports, hobbies, girls—all typical guy talk.

Suddenly Frank looked at me and asked, "What did you come to tell me?"

And for some reason it seemed natural to bring out my pocket Testament and tell him what the Lord meant to me. He nodded and then surprised me: he knew the Bible better than I did. I would mention a verse, and he would quote it accurately. I couldn't do that; I had to look them up.

Something was clearly wrong here. From what I saw on TV, all guys in jail were supposed to be cold, hard, and snarling, caring nothing for anything good, especially God. Frank was hesitant but friendly, he looked and talked like a hundred guys I'd known on the outside. Obviously he had been to church —as it turned out, longer than I had.

When the officer returned to announce we would have to break it off for dinner, I could not believe how quickly the time had gone; we had been talking for two hours.

"Are you coming again?" Frank asked as I stood up to leave.

I hesitated. I had not planned to; this was strictly a one-time event to meet, an obligation pressed on me by others. "Yes," I finally said. "I'd like that. I'll be back."

And I've been going back ever since, to youth institutions and detention centers across the nation. A one-day visit eventually grew into a special ministry of Youth For Christ with troubled kids across the world, involving thousands of volunteer men and women giving of themselves to make a big difference in the lives of kids who need a second chance.

The institution was delighted to have me visiting and easing the tensions of their young, serious offenders. As a volunteer "chaplain," I could come and go at will. One thing was sure, I was learning a lot more about life several afternoons a week at the jail than I ever did sitting in a classroom reading a sociology text.

When I returned to the jail, Frank said I should meet Leo. Leo was worth meeting and quite different from Frank. Short, wiry, outgoing, this fiery Italian youth could have been the life of any party. But he also had a fierce temper. One day he got mad at the prison barber, who was not cutting his hair right, and threw a shaving mug at him; he missed the barber but shattered a mirror. A guard asked me to see what I could do with Leo and his temper before he got into really big trouble.

I told Leo to hold his anger in until my visiting days and then take it out on me. I did not mean physically, of course. But I told him he could scream and rave all he wanted to in the counseling room. He took me up on it; the first time he was sounding off, several guards rushed in to see if I was still alive. I assured them it was all right, that Leo was just letting off steam in an acceptable way. They left shaking their heads.

Gradually I got Leo to think about more responsible ways of dealing with frustration. "If you go around giving everybody a piece of your mind, soon you won't have any pieces left," I argued. He laughed, got the point, and started to listen.

Over time I shared how the Lord could become real to both Frank and Leo. Frank needed to do something more than just know Bible portions drilled into his head as a child without much meaning, and Leo needed to learn the very basics of the Bible and its message of both forgiveness and spirit-control.

Both young men responded.

Frank went to trial first and was sentenced to life imprisonment for murder. I was in court with him and his mother when the decision was announced: "The court has found you guilty, and you are hereby sentenced to prison for the remainder of your natural life."

Frank was calm and confident in his faith as he heard these words, but a *Vancouver Sun* reporter wrote: "The young killer was unemotional and uncaring as the sentence was announced." That wasn't true. Frank was very remorseful over the tragedy, but by the time the case ended, he had accepted the Lord's forgiveness and was learning to forgive himself, which is always much harder. He was determined to make the best of his situation, even when he heard it would be life in prison. But, of course, the media sleuths never bothered to talk to him or find out how Frank actually felt; they just rushed off to file a story before deadline.

I hurried back to the prison knowing Leo would have a strong reaction when word reached him of Frank's sentence. And Leo did. He was devastated and felt that his own case was now hopeless. And it might have been except for a surprising turn of events.

Leo had killed his girlfriend Nancy in a rage. They were fighting after her parents left the two of them alone at her house. Leo's attorney, whom I met and deeply respected, suggested I visit the victim's family.

"Are you sure that's a good idea?" I replied. "If they find I'm working with the man who killed their daughter, they aren't going to be too interested. And who would blame them?"

"Go and see them," he insisted. So I did and met two compassionate, grieving parents. They loved their daughter very much, but—and this was the surprise—they loved Leo almost as much.

"He's grown up around our family," Nancy's mother explained. "When we came home that terrible night and found our daughter, Leo was one of the first people we called after phoning the police and the rest of the family. He came over and was crying with us. A police officer noticed blood on his shoes and started questioning him. Soon he was arrested. It was almost as big a blow to us as Nancy's death.

"We figured something had to be terribly wrong for him to do such a thing, even in a fit of rage. Just trying him for murder won't bring our daughter back and won't answer our questions about why it happened. So my husband and I have told Leo's attorney we will pay for a thorough psychiatric examination by the best doctor that is available. We want some answers."

The mother's voice wavered. "I dread the trial. Leo's lawyer told us the prosecutor might well show me pictures of our daughter's body at the murder scene while I'm on the witness stand. There are other ways to identify her for the court, but this way I will almost surely break down, and it will emotionally impact the jury against Leo. But I guess that's what they want."

Nancy's parents got the psychiatric report from a top expert in the field of violent behavior. That doctor came to court and in vivid detail outlined the mental deficiency in Leo that caused the youth to lose control and be unable to contain his actions.

Meanwhile, Leo had a birthday and the Youth For Christ office staff wanted to reach out to him. None of them had met Leo, but day by day they had prayed for him; from my reports they felt they knew him. They wrote him notes of encouragement and were delighted when he responded. For his birthday the staff women baked a chocolate cake—his favorite. We had a good laugh at the office when they joked about putting hacksaw blades and a knife in it.

I had permission to take the cake to Leo, and he was thrilled, cutting it and sharing it with the other young men on his tier. Shortly after I left, I got an urgent message to return immediately. I wondered what had happened in such a short time. When Leo got me in an office alone, he said, "You better return these to your office." He handed me a blade and a small knife covered with chocolate. The staff had actually done what they said as a joke! It was no joke to me, and we had one very serious staff meeting as fast as I could get back downtown. I still shudder when I think what might have happened if those weapons had got around the cell block. Leo had not thought for a moment of keeping them or even passing them on to another inmate. He *was* making progress.

At his trial the medical testimony was useful in reducing Leo's murder charge to a manslaughter conviction, and he was sentenced to seventeen years in prison. The victim's parents had shown a concern for the accused that was as amazing as it was rare, and they had saved a young man's life.

INDUCTION AND BASIC TRAINING

Shortly afterward I received an invitation from the chaplain of Green Hill Training School in Chehalis, Washington, to conduct the first spiritual emphasis week services in any area correctional center. Green Hill was not a prison but a facility designed, and a staff anxious, to redirect young offenders—a comparatively open institution ideally designed for the kind of ministry I wanted to see developed.

The meetings went well, and the base of my ministry soon transferred to Washington state. Moving from Canada to the U.S. in 1951 was an important transition. As a young immigrant (I was only seventeen) my sponsors were Washington Governor Arthur Langlie and prominent Seattle Christian businessman and musician Hilding Halvorsen. Youth For Christ leaders were taking increasing note of the outreach to offenders and for several years kept me busy visiting cities across the nation to start similar work.

Part of God's plan during this time was to give me some basic training that I would need for the years to follow. In particular, two crises came at the same time, each complicating the other.

First, I fell in love with a beautiful young American; I wanted to get married and start a family. Though a busy schedule of study and travel did not make pursuing this goal very easy, we both were determined to make it work . . . at least I thought that was the situation.

Second, there was opposition building within my own organization. Some of the leaders thought ministering to troubled kids in correctional institutions was not really the business of YFC. Others thought the ministry was a good idea but that I was too young and inexperienced to lead it. Oddly enough, my strongest support kept coming from the secular authorities with whom I worked. *They* wanted the program, and most of them supported me.

I *was* young with much to learn, and I made some mistakes. For one thing, because I was so close in age to many of these young offenders, it was easy to get too emotionally involved with some of the kids and their concerns. I did not have the experience to know how to care and yet rest the results in God's hands. Also, because of my inexperience, I tried to institute some organizational changes without considering or going through appropriate channels, which grated on some staff members.

It was a time of intense soul-searching and frustration for me as I faced real opposition and crucial choices in my own life for the first time. Far from rejoicing in what God was doing, I was so discouraged that I was ready to give up the whole ministry. Maybe my family had been right all along. Maybe I should just go back to Canada and enter the business world. But God had other ideas, and He deliberately went about showing me that He was still in control.

Settling My Marital Status

I was still planning to be married until one night my fiancée and I had a serious talk about our future plans. I listened carefully.

"Gordon," she said, "I want a husband who will stay home and be with me, not travel all over the country. You're gone so much of the time! And I don't really want to share my future husband with a bunch of juvenile delinquents."

As her words sank in, it was one of the saddest moments of my life. I realized I had to make a choice between the young lady I loved and the work I felt the Lord wanted me to do.

I cried, "God, why are You doing this to me?" But there was no sudden or dramatic answer—just a reminder that He had given me a task to perform and that He had not altered it.

Our engagement was broken. But perhaps as important, I did some careful evaluation over the next few months. I did not want to go through that heartbreak again. Perhaps I would someday meet a young lady who would share my vision for the kids. But I also knew that if I followed the path I believed God had set me on, I *would* be away many nights and during odd hours. I could not just leave my family to fend for itself simply because I was out saving the world. I had seen too many unhappy marriages and frustrated children whose crusading daddies had neglected them to serve the Lord. I did not want to do the same.

After a man's walk with the Lord, his family must come next. That is divine order and common sense, and it can certainly be done when a person is committed to heed this godly wisdom. But another route is outlined in 1 Corinthians 7. In that chapter, which stresses appropriate relationships between men and women, Paul wrote, "Now to the unmarried . . . I say: It is good for them to stay unmarried, as I am" (v. 8). This is not a command but simply wisdom about the responsibilities and concerns a family can bring. For me it was a choice, and I made it. No one urged me to remain single—quite the opposite. Many friends said I was just overreacting to breaking up with my fiancée; I would soon change my mind when I met another young lady. But that was not the case; I made a decision I believe was for the best in my life and the work to which God had called me. I have never married.

"Aren't you terribly lonely being single?" I am sometimes asked. No. There is a great difference between being alone and being lonely. I cannot recall ever feeling really lonely; a quiet evening away from the pressures and demands of my work reading a book is a rare treat that I highly treasure. The Lord has more than made up to me in satisfaction whatever I may have lost in not having a wife and family. I have no regrets.

DEALING WITH CRITICS

As I mentioned earlier, my second crisis was in learning how to deal with critics. The Bible warns us: "Woe to you when all men speak well of you" (Luke 6:26). That is one *beware* in the Bible I have not had to worry about!

At a ministerial meeting in Tacoma, Washington, a prominent pastor told a group of us that his church would not take part in a united youth crusade if the black churches were invited. I was both shocked and concerned; I could see the project falling apart. A wiser, more experienced pastor sitting nearby saw my distress, wrote a note, and handed it to me. It said, "If they don't help you when they're for you, they'll never hurt you when they're against you." Now there was good counsel for any number of situations, including my personal troubles.

God has a way of bringing good people along just when I need them. My critics were fighting my ministry and me, and frankly I was totally discouraged. A friend offered me a good job in a secular company, and I was about to take it. I remember sitting in my car along the highway near the Washington state capital at Olympia and saying, "God, they're ganging up on me. And I can't take much more."

"Is that right?" the Spirit seemed to reply. "Have you read Job lately? Or remember what happened to Joseph when he was sold into slavery in a strange land or to Daniel cast in the lions' den or to the disciples of Jesus who died for their faith?"

I never made the job interview. A few days later I went over the whole situation with my pastor. He heard my tale of woe and then replied, "So you're thinking of quitting, are you? That's just what your critics want." Then he gave me some straight advice.

"If you've done something wrong, make it right. If you're on the wrong track, turn around. But when the critics are wrong, don't listen to them. Remember what Nehemiah replied when his enemies wanted to pull him into a meeting so they could corner him: 'I am carrying on a great project and cannot go down. Why should the work stop while I leave it and go down to you?' (Nehemiah 6:3). Your critics didn't call you into the Lord's service; don't let them take you out."

So I made another decision. There is a sense of victory when an issue is settled even while the storm is still raging. I was going on, not out. And that has been my resolve ever since.

COPING WITH DANGER

Anyone working in a correctional institution knows that he or she may one day be in danger, and this was something I had to confront before I completed the basic training the Lord had for me.

One winter evening I was alone with a group of young men in a correctional center cottage. A scuffle broke out across the room far away from the phone, so I ran over to break it up. Suddenly the pair turned on me and were joined by a number of their fellows. They threw me to the floor and held me down. The fight had been a fake, a diversion to get me away from the door and the phone. As I was held, several of the young men tore strips from a sheet and used them to tie me. The keys to the front door of the unit were quickly pulled from my pocket. But that was not enough; one of the guys had a crude, sharp knife fashioned out of a piece of metal from a bed frame, and he wanted to kill me.

I was gulping what I thought was my last breath when I heard someone say: "No, we don't hurt this guy. We want to get out, not pick up a murder rap."

The first guy persisted, and finally the two of them exchanged blows. I lay helplessly on the floor, looking up at two guys fighting over whether I lived or died. Finally the second youth landed a heavy blow that sent the first one sprawling across the floor.

"Now get up and do what I tell you," said my rescuer. "We leave him alone, and we go through that front door. Let's get out of here and right now!"

They smashed through the door and ran in all directions, fourteen escapees. But because there was no real plan for what to do once they escaped, they were all rounded up in a few hours by alert police.

I told the officials what happened, and they prepared attempted murder charges against the two ringleaders—one of them the guy who saved my life. I later visited him in an isolation cell and thanked him for helping me that fateful night. He frankly told me there wasn't anything personal in his help; he just did not want a murder charge.

I told him he would have to answer for the escape in court, but I would testify for him and tell the judge exactly what his role had been. He was subsequently found not guilty on the attempted murder charge.

In my ministry there are often times when I face dangerous situations; I don't like them, but I know the Lord is with me and caring for me. I have been caught in a prison riot but left unharmed. And I have seen the bloody, brutalized victims of gang violence in a number of institutions. Yet I go back because that is where the Lord wants me; there is a job to be done and a message to be shared. The confidence comes from knowing I am where God wants me to be and that He has promised to be with me no matter what happens.

Dealing with Discouragement

As I have ministered to kids in trouble, not all have responded. I took that personally at first until I read of Jesus' disappointing encounter with the rich young ruler who learned the truth but turned away (Luke 18). I met that young man's counterpart.

Lee was a bright, friendly teenager from Spokane, Washington, serving out a commitment at Green Hill Training School when I met him. His history was rough: a broken home, an abusive and alcoholic father, too many foster homes, in and out of detention centers, and a record of increasingly serious arrest charges.

Still he came to some of our group meetings, and I often talked with him alone. But it was obvious that, while our relationship was firm and friendly, he was not about to accept what I was saying concerning how the Lord could change his life. One night he spelled it out to me.

"Gordon, you and I are friends. I hope we always will be. But you need to know I'm not going to get converted, become a Christian, or however else you want to describe it. You and I are on two different paths, going two different directions. I wish it could be different, but it isn't."

I tried to tell him God's love is long and patient. But he waved his hand to silence me. "I've made my choice. It's not going to change, not now or ever. So maybe you'd better put your time in with some guys who will listen."

A short time later I learned that Lee escaped from the institution, stole several cars, and was finally caught in Montana. He had hitchhiked a ride with a traveling salesman, killed the man, and taken his car before being captured at a roadblock.

A few years later Lee was one of the principal leaders in a prison riot. He shot and killed the deputy warden before national guard sharp-shooters ended his life.

Certainly not every youth who does not respond to the gospel ends up dying in a prison riot, but it is a serious thing to trifle with the sacred, and it is sad to see a person—any person—make that choice.

But the disappointment of seeing someone reject the Lord and choose the way of death has been redeemed many times by the joy of seeing others respond to the gospel and begin caring for others. For instance, although Montana was the scene of the tragic death of one young man, it was also where another youth had an irreplaceable impact on my thinking.

Ira was fifteen when he was sent to the Montana Industrial School at Miles City for his involvement with an older boy and girl in a robbery-murder. He was a quiet, hard-working young man, well-liked by the staff, and he especially enjoyed his assignment on the school farm.

He came to our Bible study groups and took an active part. My friend Franklin Robbie (who later developed the Yellowstone Ranch for delinquent youth in Billings) and I both got to know and appreciate Ira. He was not a demonstrative kid, but when he came to the Lord his faith was sincere, genuine, and quiet.

One day a secretary at our Great Falls office showed me a letter from Ira with one dollar enclosed for our ministry. I took the dollar and a few weeks later confronted Ira.

"I really appreciate the gift you sent, Ira, but we can't keep it. I know how hard you have to work to earn even a few cents here, and you need it. So I'm giving it back to you."

There were tears in his eyes, and he refused to take the bill in my open hand. "Mr. McLean, I didn't give it to you. It's not yours to give back. I gave it to the Lord so other guys will hear about Him, maybe before they end up like I did. Take it back. Use it like I wrote you."

There was nothing more to say. I stumbled over an apology and did as he directed. The young people I meet have taught me many lessons; in truth there are many times I receive a good deal more than I give.

MOVING ON

After basic training took me from Chehalis, Washington, to Montana, and back to Tacoma, Washington, I spent fifteen years in San José, California, working with Bay Area street gangs. Then, in 1982, the Lord sent me to Chicago with the assignment of ministering to kids in confinement and following them up on some of the most dangerous streets in America. I had seen what the Lord could do in Washington, Montana, and California. Still, as I headed for Chicago, I thought, "If the Lord can work there and with those young people, He can work anyplace." I would soon find out.

3

On the Streets

Two youths leaned against the brick storefront across the street as they watched me take pictures of some kids on a corner in southwest Chicago. Both observers were about fourteen, with their bicycles at their feet. As soon as I noticed them, one motioned for me to come across.

"What'cha doin'?" he challenged.

I had just arrived in Chicago to begin a new ministry with Metro Chicago Youth For Christ. Why this forceful kid, whose street name turned out to be Satan (but whose real name was Jason), could not tell what I was doing with my Minolta pointed at my subjects only a few feet away, I could not imagine. But I answered in as friendly a manner as I could: "Just taking some pictures."

"Of *them*?" he asked. "They're nothin'!"

"And who," I inquired, "is everything?"

"We are! Most of those guys are just wannabes.¹ The rest are toasted. We rule this hood. We're the Two-Six Nation!"

This kid really was impressed with power, but to call his gang a "nation" seemed a little grandiose to me. Later, I learned that gangs are called nations largely because the world of street youths is very limited; they do not know much about anywhere

1. They "want-to-be" real gang members.

else. The Two-Six Nation is named after 26th Street on the south side of Chicago.

There are 125 gangs on Chicago streets, some very small in number, just a handful of kids hanging out on a street corner. Others are large, the largest being the Black Gangsters and its spin-offs with 10,000 members, a figure that includes kids all the way from hard-core "gangbangers" to those who identify with a group because it dominates their neighborhood but who are really not involved. *Gangbangers* is the term they use for themselves, not to be confused with the former use of the term describing a *group* sexual assault on a woman.

New York City kids will gangbang in the assaultive sense, but they call it *wilding.* Detroit gangs, on the other hand, consider themselves advanced beyond petty street rivalry. There the main gangs—the Young Boys, Inc., and Pony Down—have graduated from being social, to being territorial, then to being delinquent, and finally to being business-oriented, drug-dealing empires raking in hundreds of millions a year. They have also reached a new all-time high for deadly violence. Gang colors[2] don't impress them, nor do flashy jewelry and big cars. Showing off money doesn't even concern them; making more of it does.

Chicago kids are more organized into gang groups that control neighborhoods, and they would consider it crude and demeaning to attack a citizen on their streets. That, of course, has not stopped the shooting deaths and wounding of innocent citizens caught between warring gangs, but the kids are most often at war with each other. Individuals attacking an outsider are usually drug-addicts in search of money for a quick fix. In fact, some gang groups are social organizations fulfilling a needed place of acceptance for kids lacking in emotional ties and a stable family. It is only when they move out of that limited role, usually because of outside pressure, that they become a menace. And that has happened to many gangs.

Jason and his partner, Little Kato, the street-corner members of the Two-Six Nation that I had just met, said that if I

2. Jackets or other items of clothing that show by color a person's gang affiliation—for example, black-and-blue, black-and-gold, purple-and-white, orange-and-black. These need not resemble the elaborately decorated "colors" of motorcycle gangs.

really wanted to see how a gang ran I should meet *their* boys. When I told them I was newly arrived from California and interested in getting to know the kids on the streets, they offered to arrange a meeting.

They were men of their word, and two nights later at the Corkery School yard, I had a preview of fifty Two-Six boys, all curious to see the preacher from California. I got lots of pictures and heard many war stories of great victories over their rivals, especially the Latin Kings, and learned quickly that they never tell you about a battle they lost, unless it was a sneak attack by an opposition that greatly outnumbered them. It was my second week in Chicago in April of 1982, and I was off to a lively start.

Laying the Groundwork

Two things enhanced the prospects of building a ministry to these kids. One was the excellent foundation that a fine Youth For Christ staff of men and women had laid with the juvenile court and probation staff, who held the YFC workers in high regard. The other was the careful and detailed briefing I received on the problems of the street from the Gang Crimes units of both the Chicago Police Department and the Cook County state's attorney's office.

Several days were devoted to simply listening and then digesting the volumes of facts and names they laid before me to give me a picture of what was happening in their jurisdictions. Certainly theirs is a crucial, tough job of dealing with the growing rate of youthful street violence. The job of policing and prosecuting young Chicago felons was more than a career choice; it is seen by these officers as a vital component of public safety. But before I seriously went to work on the streets there was an important call I needed to make.

Over at the county jail, I asked a chaplain to arrange for me to meet with David, still in his teens at the time and described by authorities as a major drug trafficker and Two-Six leader. David had crowded considerable living and several tragedies into his teenage years. He had seen his father, brother, and cousin all killed, leaving him as the key man on the street long before he wanted that responsibility.

I had no way of evaluating his history or reputation, so I simply took him as I met him at the jail: a friendly, intelligent, well-built, perceptive young man. As we talked in a jail office, he asked me why I had moved from California. He did not think anyone in his right mind ever left the West Coast, especially to come to Chicago, and I must admit that at times I would have to agree with him. But at that moment I answered, "I want to build contacts with kids on Chicago streets so I can help them come to know the Lord and do positive things with their lives."

"What do you mean, 'positive things'?"

"You know: family, education, jobs."

"Well, what do you want from me?"

"I've met some of your friends out there," I answered, "and you could certainly make it easier by calling some of the key guys you know and suggesting they cooperate with me."

Without hesitation he picked up the office phone, made a few calls, and told me who the young men were with whom he had talked. So I left with three new contacts and David to thank for putting me in touch with them. As persons of influence on the street, they proved invaluable to the ministry. I also met David's family, who were very gracious people, and one of his attorneys, John DeLeon, who remains one of our closest friends and wisest consultants.

A Dose of Hard Reality

It did not take me long to learn that life on the streets and in the justice system is unpredictable, and ministry to these kids does not guarantee storybook endings.

David was later convicted on charges that he gave orders resulting in two murders. He is still appealing his sentence of life imprisonment. His trial was my first introduction to the Chicago court system. When the evidence fell short of mandating "guilt beyond a reasonable doubt," the prosecutors cried out against "these gang members" and demanded "we send a message to the streets that we won't tolerate gangs. . . . Make our streets safe again."

The technique worked and continues to work. The weaker the facts in a case the louder and more pointed this send-a-message argument becomes. It succeeds because the average juror is terrified by the word "gangs" and can't or won't evaluate any evidence once the accused is associated with a gang.

Justice for street kids is a far cry from what is described in civics books or taught in law school. To the suburbanite, "guilty" is a moral condemnation and a disgrace, but not to street kids. Most often it is what the man downtown in the black robe says when your luck runs out. "Guilty" is the decision handed down by the jury or judge, which may or may not be the actual case. Sometimes the guilty verdict is understood by all (though rarely verbalized) as "maybe not guilty in this instance but probably guilty some other time, so we'll let it stand." Witnesses from a rival gang may testify just to get an enemy off their backs. Or real witnesses are intimidated not to show up, and a guilty gang member goes free.

At the juvenile center, one of the first kids I met was Tony, a young Puerto Rican. Tony wanted me to teach him all I could about the Bible, and he in turn took on the task of adding to my knowledge of the streets. Both while he was confined and later after his release, Tony was my unfailing guide. He introduced me to his Puerto Rican Stone buddies, an approach that has become standard procedure when kids who are released take our staff and me to their neighborhoods and help us get acquainted. It seldom matters to the gang who we are. As long as we are friends of someone like Tony, we are accepted by the others.

Tony made good progress, settled down, did well in his Bible reading, and got into a G.E.D. program to complete his high school education. I had great hopes for him when he got out of detention.

But one Friday night Tony did not make it home from his girlfriend's place just a few blocks away. He was shot and killed by rivals who spotted him alone and unguarded. Instead of his graduation, I attended his funeral, the first of many in Chicago where I mourned with hurting family and friends.

Mapping the Gangs

I met Gallo about the same time, who claimed that the Latin Kings organization, of which he is a part, was the greatest organization on the street. He was down[3] for the gold-and-

3. Dedicated gang member.

black and the five-point star that distinguished his group from the six-point star of the opposition. His family eventually moved away from gang-centered streets to a better neighborhood, but by then it was too late to rescue Gallo. He had made his choice.

When the move was decided, Gallo told me, "We're moving next week to a nice suburb. I'll have a new chapter of the Kings started there within a month."

And he did. So a nice community that never experienced street wars was suddenly brought into it by a family eager to move their son away from the tragedies, only to find that they took the problems with them. Gallo also came back regularly to the old neighborhood to keep in touch with his boys.

Some gangs I met are merely social groups, others are into violence, and still more are manipulated by older adult criminals involved in drug sales. The danger comes as a group moves from the first category up the line. Similar danger results when police and schools react as if all the kids in the first group are in the other two categories. Too frequently I see official blindness destroy kids, kicking them out of school or treating them as hardened criminals when they are not. When kids are labeled as desperate and dangerous, unfortunately that is what many become. Kids have an amazing propensity to live up to adult predictions—whether good or bad.

Chicago youth gangs are divided into two deadly, rival federations: *Folks* and *People*. *Folks* are recognized by graffiti that include a six-pointed star. They wear caps with the bill turned to the right. When they stand with their arms crossed, it is always left arm over the right. *People* are identified by a five-pointed star, caps to the left, and right arm over the left. There are gangs of all races on both sides, and all but a very few gangs—such as the Gaylords and Jousters—identify with one of these two federations.

Frequently there are wars within a side, but there is always war across the two groupings, and often it is the side more than the race that matters. Blacks and Latinos will fight both races of opposition members. Caucasians do not matter much in the gang structure and are not considered heavyweights on the streets—much to their chagrin. Among predominately white gangs are the Simon City Royals, Gaylords (who are neither gay nor lords), and the Insane Popes (not a group of mad Catholics as their name might imply; POPES means "Protect Our People, Eliminate Spooks, Spicks, and Scum"; they don't have many friends). There are even a few skinheads around, though it is generally considered that they have as little under their scalp as on top. Strident racism and white supremacy is not popular on the streets.

Most gangs within the federations are highly territorial. Wearing your colors or jacket on another gang's turf is a quick way to get killed. Even wearing a cap tilted the wrong direction is dangerous. Carefully marked graffiti on a wall of a school or other building delineates the territory of a gang. Gang control can change from block to block or even from one side of a street to the other.

WHY KIDS JOIN GANGS

I found kids joining gangs as young as seven or eight years of age. If they're still alive at seventeen, they're survivors. Some kids get pressured into joining, but most volunteer for two reasons: protection or action. "Protection from what?" one might ask. The loner on the street will most likely be physically or sexually abused. The gang member will not; he has his group for protection. The rare pervert who tries to molest a gang youth usually ends up losing—probably his life.

In the inner-city, where options are few, gang life provides excitement. Today's street kids are not just pulling pranks or loading up on five-finger discounts at the local mall. They are cool and tough, some of the sharpest leaders in their community—sadly being wasted in dangerous and useless pursuits. The discipline they respect does not come from their homes or the courts but from gang peers where punishment for violations of gang rules and loyalty is often firm and swift, virtues frequently lacking in the official system. Discipline is a real attraction of the gangs.

Money is, of course, another motive for joining a street gang. The El Rukins, once known as the Blackstone Rangers, claims that its organization is only interested in personal and community betterment—and legitimate financial investments. They have had extensive property holdings, but many neigh-

borhood residents and law enforcement officials believe these
are fronts for drug sales and other illegal ventures.

The African-American youths I know are raised in a ghetto
or housing project, usually by a mother alone who cannot cope
with a growing teenager. He joins a gang to find a family and a
sense of belonging.

The Hispanic youths I have met are very proud of being
Latino but grow up with parents who have come to the U.S.
from either Puerto Rico or Mexico and remain more comfortable with the language and values of the homeland. The family
is normally intact, but the children grow up in new surround-
ings, boasting of their Latino heritage and yet eager to be
Americanized—Big Macs®, cars, Levis®, ghetto blasters—and
the result is both a language and culture gap between parents
and children.

These five things often constitute the primary reasons kids
join gangs: protection, action, money, a sense of family and
belonging, and the desire to bridge a cultural gap. Of course,
becoming a gangbanger does not appear to accomplish Ameri-
canization in a very effective way. But to the kid on the street,
it has more appeal than one might think. Many of these kids
are provincial. Television is their only window on the rest of
America.[4] Certainly the America they see there is depicted by
violence and crime as much as it is by suburbia and order. For
them, suburbia is far away and unreal, whereas street action is
real and close at hand.

What a shame that the appeal of gangs starts as a search for
a family, a sense of belonging, finding someone who cares and
understands. *The gang becomes an illegitimate means of meeting
legitimate needs.* A suburban youth gains his or her acceptance
from sports, activities, the arts, student government, and the
honor roll. Too many inner-city youths—often the sharpest and
brightest of the lot—gain their recognition on the streets.

WHAT ABOUT THE GIRLS?

There are a few girls' gangs, but mostly the girls function
as auxiliaries to the boys' groups: Latin Queens, Lady Two-Six-
es, Lady Disciples, the Flowers, and so on. The girls can be

4. TV watching becomes a tranquilizer to deaden the pain of an empty life.

vicious fighters and are often used to carry the boys' weapons to the scene of a battle.

Girls are not so often involved in the type of law violations that the boys are arrested for. Consequently on any given day there are some 500 boys in the Juvenile Detention Center in Chicago and *maybe* 25 girls. At Cook County Jail there will be 7,500 men but only 450 women. Girls tend to have more personal problems such as family relationships and boy/girl problems.

Most of the girls are from impoverished homes and neighborhoods and suffer from a poor self-image. Too often the single mother dominates, and she usually became pregnant with the goal of forcing a man to love her by mothering his child. It rarely works. White or black, with few exceptions, out-of-wedlock teenage pregnancy dooms both mother and child to lives of dependency. These children of children show high rates of infant mortality; they are more neglected and abused; they typically do poorly in school and frequently wind up as teenage parents themselves.

"It multiplies," said a teacher at an inner-city school. "We have children living in chaos, and they grow up and have children living in chaos." The girls can be told to get out of their home and have their boyfriend take care of them. In some cases the pressures can be enormous.

But fortunately, rather than being gang affiliated, many girls become our best allies in trying to get their boyfriends off dangerous streets. Rosa's boyfriend, for instance, was an active Latin King. He was torn between his love for her and loyalty to his boys on the street. But she would not let up. "It's either them or me," she insisted. "I want you to finish school, get a job, and settle down. Then we can get married and start a family." She won, but it took a very persistent and determined young lady with a good deal of conviction and courage to make it. They are now settled down, and he is off the streets. Rosa may well have saved his life.

It's Hard to Stay Out

Richard's older brothers hardly set a good example for him. Several have been in prison, and one is on death row fighting a conviction in a gang-related killing of three youths. But Richard had no part in any of those problems. A good-looking youth, fine student, and excellent athlete, he wanted no part of the gang life on the streets in his northside Chicago neighborhood. He was a junior high school boy, serious about his grades, playing football, enjoying a good time with the girls. Trouble? Gangs? Drugs? Forget it. He saw what happened to his brothers and was determined not to follow them. He would be different and make his parents proud.

And he did well until he started Lakeview High School near his home, in the territory of a gang that was a rival to his brothers'. When the Eagles found out through their grapevine of informants (usually girls) who his brothers were, they brought the battle to Richard.

He was harassed, insulted, jeered, punched, even shot at. Still he would not give in. Whatever quarrel they had with his brothers was not his. But he protested to no avail. Like it or not, he was a prime target. Concerned school staff seemed helpless to intervene, especially when the pattern of terror continued even away from the campus. Even the police who regularly patrol city schools could not protect him from determined, ongoing gang attacks.

One day gang members surrounded the football practice field waiting for him to leave. The coach went with Richard to the principal, and the three of them reviewed the situation. The principal is a compassionate, caring woman who wanted to help Richard, but she realized the seriousness of the problem.

"All we can do is guarantee your safety *in* this school. If you're not safe going to and from school, maybe you'll have to transfer to another high school," she concluded sadly.

Richard understood, and he made the switch—only to have the problems resurface in a few weeks. The local boys' and girls' clubs even tried to help Richard, but wherever he went the opposition continued their verbal threats and physical attacks.

Finally, in desperation, Richard broke. He sought out Insane Eddie, a leader of the gang in his hood and announced he was joining. Eddie rejected the idea and told Richard not to get involved. But Richard insisted. If he was going to be constantly harassed because a rival gang could not separate him from his brothers' reputation, then so be it. He'd make his own "rep."

Eddie told me what was happening and said the situation really bothered him. "Richard belongs in school, not out here," Eddie said and urged me to do what I could to divert the youth to other channels. I did track Richard down, and we talked about what he was going through, but I had one bitter, angry youth on my hands who was in no mood to listen to anyone's counsel.

The result was quick and tragic. A few nights later Richard came across a youth he presumed to be a rival, pulled out a gun, and fired. The young man died and his girlfriend was wounded. The gang insisted to me and everyone else that the deceased was not one of their members.

Richard was charged with murder and placed in the youth section of the county jail. Here I saw him again, this time a broken, discouraged, frightened kid who handled a street problem in the only way he thought he could, and his choice could not have been more wrong.

Forgiveness, repentance, and new life were words he very much needed to hear. Richard came to our services at the jail and heard these words from the only genuine source—God's Word. It took quite a while for Richard to work through his feelings and the tremendous load of guilt he carried before he could ask God's forgiveness. But he finally gave his life to God and began the more difficult process of forgiving himself.

Eventually he was released on bail. Now quite a different young man than had been on the streets a few months earlier, he was more like a student-athlete than a street warrior.

In spite of the change in Richard, there remained a very tough question: where to put him in school? He couldn't attend any school in his neighborhood or anywhere he was known. So we decided on a unique strategy, enrolling him in a school in another part of the city dominated by his rival's friends—the last place his enemies would think to look for him. The principal was cooperative, and I even talked quietly with some gang kids in the school I knew and enlisted their help. They could not believe we were actually placing an enemy on their campus, especially one who had killed someone he thought was an ally of theirs. But they said they would look out for him. They kept their word, and things worked out—for a while.

Meanwhile, Richard was regularly active in church, attending Bible class and thoroughly enjoying the services. The congregation knew who he was, but it did not seem to matter; he was now one of *them*, and he was surrounded by loving, caring people. This was church at its best. Richard often spoke to youth groups, churches, service clubs, and later on TV with Dr. James Kennedy. On every occasion Richard left a clear-cut, well-spoken testimony for the Lord.

Then a brazen young rival phoned Richard and told him he would not have to face trial—he would be dead long before the court date. Richard told the caller that if he was so anxious to get to him, then he would arrange a meeting. Richard also invited his rival to church. The kid was so surprised that he met with Richard and got to see firsthand the change in his life. He also went to church with Richard one Sunday evening.

In this way Richard made friends with a few of his enemies, but it was not possible to conciliate all of them. The result was a serious setback.

Still Haunted by the Past

A young lady, who was a close friend of his enemies, transferred into Richard's new high school from the old neighborhood. She was amazed to find him there but told him she would keep his secret. She kept it only until she got back to the old neighborhood that evening and passed the news to Richard's enemies.

They made their plans quickly, contacting their gang allies at the new school. The next day he was quickly surrounded and threatened. In a panic, he broke through the crowd and ran up the street to the house of a friend who gave him a gun. He ran back to catch a bus home but was headed off by the rivals. When they again confronted him, he pulled out the gun and ordered them to stand back. He was sweating and scared, but he did not fire. He ran through the crowd and threw the gun on the roof of a low entranceway as the police drove up to arrest him.

He was back in jail on a gun possession charge, re-arrested while he was out waiting trial for a murder. It did not look good no matter what the circumstances. One positive factor was the attorney representing him—Richard Kling, a law professor at Kent School of Law—who normally handles only the most serious death penalty cases and uses his courtroom assignments as teaching opportunities for his students. He was representing Richard's brother on death row, so he took the case of the younger boy as a favor to the family.

However, there was little doubt of the facts in Richard's case, and he was found guilty. A sensitive judge, concerned for the young man when the whole picture of what happened was before him, did as much as he could with the sentencing restrictions placed upon him. Richard was given twenty-eight years in prison.

His troubles were not over. A young man in prison faces pressures and threats and temptations that few people in the free world can even begin to understand. If he wants to align himself with troublemakers and be a hardened criminal, then the path in confinement is easily and quickly laid out. That was not Richard's choice. He was assaulted by a prison guard and placed in segregation when he resisted. Today he is older, maturing in every area of his life, strong in his walk with the Lord, and determined to come out of the experience a better and stronger man.

"Without the Lord, I would have no hope and would never have changed. With Him I know I am going to make it," Richard has firmly declared. And the people who know him best believe he is correct.

As I have gotten to know kids like Richard, become more familiar with the pressures of growing up in the inner city, caught a glimpse of gang life and the total identity it generates, I have gradually begun to realize that I have entered a different world.

4

Different Worlds

Not long ago I was speaking to the high school group at Christ Church of Oak Brook, which serves an affluent area west of Chicago. As an ice-breaker, each teenager described the biggest crisis he or she had faced in the last week:

"My folks grounded me for the whole weekend."

"My Dad wouldn't let me have the car for an important date."

"My steady boyfriend broke up with me."

"I'm worried about my grades."

"Harvard didn't accept my college application."

"I wasn't invited to the Cotillion sponsored by the country club."

I don't want to trivialize these crises, but they certainly are different from those faced by kids on the street. I whispered to Jeunesse, a young black Vice Lord from urban Chicago who had come with me, "When I introduce you, tell them about *your* biggest crisis this past week."

He did: "Last Friday I heard gun shots and ran outside my house. There in the middle of the cold, rainy street lay my best friend, bleeding. I rushed out and threw my coat over him, hardly noticing that bullets were still flying from a carload of rivals who had turned VanNess Avenue into a shooting gallery.

I yelled back to my mom to call the police and an ambulance. Luckily they got there in time to save my friend's life."

Admittedly, the suburban church has to make a special effort to understand the world of the gang member. We do live in different worlds, even if they are only a few miles apart, and suburbanites—at least those who see their biggest problems as how to lose weight or where to park the car—may find it hard to understand the agony of daily, raw violence with no place to hide.

For the kid on the streets, each day is a fight for survival, and survival often requires fronting.[1] Of course, adults use fronts too. But it is an exhausting, dangerous practice no matter who does it. In a drama prepared by students at the county jail school for teens from the community, they described their life:

> "Fronting, like an ice-cold wall, pretend to be something you're not at all. Trying to be hard but you're soft inside. Gangster Man. Superhuman with his imaginary little gun. Take a close look at his hand. It's not a gun he's holding. It's his fate. That's the problem with a front. At first you can drop it. But later you lose track. You can't remember what's front and what's you.
>
> Gang thing makes you think you got something. It comes down on you like a spell. You think the fear is gone. You think the guilt is gone. You go in as deep as you can. It's like you've gone into this long tunnel. So long as you're in that tunnel you feel like you can do anything. Everybody's scared of me, man. Ain't nobody can touch me."

Getting popped[2] bursts the bubble and jail is no picnic.

> "Man, the nights are the worst. Sometimes I just lay awake and think deep, think hard. I think, why am I like this? How did I end up in this place? For a moment I can almost understand what's going on with me. Then it fades and I don't understand anything. I cry, man. I just lay there and cry."

One of the hardest things to understand about life on the streets is the difficulty of escaping it.

1. Putting up a false front, pretending to be what one is not.
2. Arrested.

ADDICTED TO THE STREETS

"Being in a street organization means being at war with the opposition and looking out for them all the time," explained Sammy, an eager mid-teen Chicago youth. "Some of the guys are into drug sales, stealing, and auto thefts. Me, I got into it following in the steps of my older brother. He's in a Florida prison serving time now, but when I was younger I looked up to him and wanted to be out where the excitement was. Soon, most of us put the streets before anything—family, school, even life itself."

Gang life is like being addicted to alcohol. The pleasure is great at first, but eventually it masters a youth, and he can't let go. Short of a miracle, he will stay in the gang until he goes to jail for a long time or dies. The gang becomes his family and demands his first loyalty. Its discipline for violators is sure, severe, and quick.

"But," as Sammy noted, "it's a life that doesn't last forever."

For him it ended abruptly in a shooting.

"At first I didn't know I was shot," Sammy told me. "I thought I just hit my arm. One of my partners saw the hole in my jacket with the blood, freaked out, and told me I had been hit."

Sammy and three of his Latin King buddies had a violent encounter with plain-clothes police officers, who the boys insist did not identify themselves until shots were fired. Sammy's bullets missed, the officers' did not.

Sammy was taken to a Humboldt Park area hospital where treating the results of gang violence is a daily affair. Other cities face the same crisis. The U.S. Army sends its doctors to Watts area hospitals in Los Angeles so they can learn firsthand how to treat combat wounds.

Sammy spent ten days recovering from an arm wound and then two months in the juvenile detention center as the charge of attempted murder of a police officer was processed against him. Later, he was sent to the Department of Corrections for an evaluation and a report back to the court.

Talking with me after he returned to the detention center, Sammy expanded on life on the streets: "I was into drug sales and gaining rank in the group so I could give orders to move out on a mission or pull a hit on the opposition. It isn't all fun and games. One of my buddies died in my arms, and I was on the scene when several others were killed. It's not fun watching your back every day, waking up wondering if today you'll make it home to see your mother again."

Sammy shook his head. "My family could travel anywhere they wanted, but I couldn't. I was locked into my gang territory. Once I was on a border street near our rivals and was shot in the foot. Even your own relatives turn against you if they are in a rival gang; that's how strong street loyalty is. Our organization has rules and policies that I can't talk about, but we're expected to know them and keep them.

"And rivals aren't the only danger," he continued. "When I went to court, the police officer told me—right in front of my mother—'We don't shoot to wound. I intended to kill you.'[3] That's scary. I realized all the crazy things I had been doing aren't worth it. All the rank, power, and money on the streets won't take the place of your life."

Oddly enough it was a street rival of Sammy's that introduced me to him in the juvenile detention center. We had a series of good talks about the Lord and how His forgiveness can change a young man's life. For Sammy, it made a difference.

"I accepted the Lord," he is now eager to say, "and that started some big changes in my life and thinking."

Sammy was released on probation and is now planning to complete high school and continue studying graphic arts. But one thing that amazes me is his testimony that "I can even respect some of my former enemies." I guess I should not be surprised; that's what God promises in Proverbs 16:7: "When a man's ways are pleasing to the Lord, he makes even his enemies live at peace with him."

Sammy is active in his church, with his family, and also in our YFC ministry. He takes part in many of our ministry presentations and was a guest of Rotary Club #1 in Chicago when the Cook County sheriff spoke on youth problems and needs.

3. "Shoot to kill" is standard police procedure due to the inherent inaccuracy of side arms, coupled with concern for the protection of police officers.

The kid who was addicted to the streets has been "detoxed" by the Lord.

"You Ain't Seen Nothin' Yet"

Sammy's story may seem a world removed from the challenges most families face. But suburban parents who cannot envision life on the streets may not be so insulated from it in the future.

The principal was proud of his high school as he showed me around. Located in a beautiful setting in a lovely Chicago suburb, the school attracts fine teachers, who in turn strive for academic excellence in the students. Its athletic teams top their leagues in several sports, and its artistic departments are widely acclaimed.

The student body historically has been largely Caucasian, but there is a growing number of African-Americans, Hispanic, and Asian students on campus. The economic range in what was once a middle-upper-class school is also more diverse, especially with additions at the lower end of the scale—not all of them racial minorities.

"There is no gang activity in this school," the principal assured me during our tour. "My staff and I are on top of the situation and plan to act quickly at the first sign of such influences among the students."

He was wrong; there are gangs on his campus. I was not sure how to tell him, but I finally suggested he take another look. There might be more problems than he suspected.

Before talking to the principal, I had talked with a street gang that was well established in the neighborhood *and* in the school; in fact, the leader and his boys met me in the school lunchroom. Earlier that same young man had driven me around the area where his rivals are situated, most of them also students at the school. Both sides are still too small to control a significant portion of the student body. They did not do graffiti around the campus, and they confine their battles to the streets at night. But when at school they screen volunteers who wanted to join. Why here? Partly to defy real or imagined societal rejection by Caucasian students.

It is a pattern I have seen all across the country. As long as the Crips and Bloods from Los Angeles or the Black Gangsters, Vice Lords, Latin Kings, and Disciples from Chicago stayed in the inner city, surrounding communities could rest easy. Smaller cities and towns, as well as rural areas farther out, considered themselves immune from the blight of youth violence.

No longer.

Many inner-city youth resent being universally labeled delinquents, gang members, or dope dealers, when the majority of them go seriously about the job of bettering themselves and rising above the disadvantages they have inherited. But serious problems are multiplying in *all* our communities. Gangs control whole neighborhoods, and innocent people are often caught between rivals and killed in the ongoing street wars. Homicides in Chicago in 1991 averaged three deaths a day, a 40 percent increase over the year before and the largest number in the city's history. Tragically, most of the victims were young people killed over drugs or gang disputes. The reports from Washington, Atlanta, Miami, Los Angeles, and Las Vegas are similar.

Discussing the increased youth homicide rate—now the principal cause of death among teens in this country—Dr. Charles Ewing of New York State University in Buffalo told WBBM news radio in Chicago, "From 1988 to 1989 the murder rate by juveniles increased 25 percent and probably will climb at least at a 10 percent rate each year for some time."[4] Ewing, a professor of law and psychology and the author of *Kids Who Kill*,[5] indicated that the biggest spread of youth violence, nearly all of it drug and gang related, has been in the smaller communities and outlying areas.

His prognosis: "It will only get worse. What we have now is bad, but frankly you ain't seen nothin' yet."

The Crips and the Bloods have spread from Los Angeles to sixty-five cities across the country, up the West Coast (which might be expected), but also as far away as Atlanta, Miami, Omaha, Minneapolis, Indianapolis, and many small communi-

4. August 5, 1990.
5. Charles Ewing, *Kids Who Kill* (Lexington, Mass.: Lexington Books, 1990).

ties that serve as drug distribution points. Even the national parks have become drug and gang targets.[6] Gangs on city streets are nothing new. In 1882, the Salvation Army was attacked by the notorious "Blades"—a thousand strong at the time—in Sheffield, England. In American cities, youth gangs began by battling for status among the have-nots. As waves of new ethnic groups arrived on the scene, there was a continued scramble for recognition and power. The weapons on the streets were most often fists and perhaps baseball bats; only later came home-made zip guns, chains, and finally small hand-guns. Over time, assimilation of these groups into the mainstream often dissolved their structures. For those who did not, youth gangs continued to provide a measure of power and self-control.

The 1960s saw a divergence from the goal of breaking into the establishment. That generation—frustrated by a bogged-down, protracted war in Vietnam and fueled too often by psychedelic drugs—wanted a political, economic, and social restructuring of the country. They, at least, had a cause for which they fought, however controversial and misunderstood their goals may have been.

But the rebels that follow them in the nineties have no cause, no goal beyond immediate, personal, material gain. Idealism has been replaced with shallow cynicism and selfishness. Kids are so defeated they do not look for a better tomorrow; they're uncertain whether there will *be* a tomorrow. They are not against materialism and the system; they just want short-cuts that help them get it all *now*. And fists and chains have been replaced by shotguns and automatic weapons in the hands of the angry and immature.

"Fist fights?" said one of my young friends when asked if kids ever "duke it out" to settle quarrels and differences. "Nah. It's guns or nothin'."

The nineties have inherited the huge wave of Hispanic young people, largely from Mexico and Puerto Rico, who came in the eighties to find their place in America along with a contingent of Asians from a wide range of countries, both educated

6. *All* fifty states and the District of Columbia now report gang activity.

immigrants and traumatized refugees. Unfortunately, the eighties were also characterized by unsettled economic conditions and large cutbacks in government programs meant to assist the disadvantaged who were trying to break into the mainstream. Of course, for most inner-city African-Americans, these cutbacks were nothing new.

Many Asian young people come from a tradition of sacrifice and hard work, strong family ties, and an appreciation for education. Being successful for these young people may be a long and difficult road, but it is possible. However, in New York City's Chinatown, the Ghost Shadows and the newer Born to Kill Gang control the streets and link up with other youth gangs in Chinese communities in Los Angeles, San Francisco, Chicago, Toronto, Vancouver, Amsterdam, Hong Kong, and Sydney. Their tactics involve robberies, extortion, and drug-trafficking. In fact, the Chinese have taken over from the Italian-dominated Mafia as the major supplier of heroin in the U.S.[7]

It is a world that is sucking in more and more of our young people.

LIFE IN THE SLAMMER

In addition to pervasive violence on the streets, the world of the gang member includes the potential, even the probability, of prison. What is life in prison really like? Riko is one inmate who can answer from his own experience.

Born in Chicago, he grew up on the streets, joining the Imperial Gangsters at age thirteen for the usual reasons: fun and friends, protection and identity. He was in juvenile detention six times for auto theft and other charges before he was sixteen. When he was arrested after that birthday, officials decided he should be tried as an adult.

He ended up at Pontiac prison for fourteen months.

"Everything I knew from the streets was there at the prison," Riko said, "only more of it and worse. They were banging as well as dealing dope. I had to constantly look out for my

---

7. Now rivaling them in crime and drugs are the Vietnamese youth gangs and the brutal Jamaican Posse.

back. I also had to play a role. I couldn't share anything with anyone else—you don't loan or borrow in prison—and I had to put on a tough, indifferent front, which was anything but what I felt inside."

He described what happens when an inmate first arrives. "The officers will set you out[8] to the guys on the main line.[9] If you're a neutron,[10] have a snitch jacket,[11] or if there are rivals out to get you, then you can go into protective custody, where you *might* be safe, but only as long as you stay there in virtual isolation.

"In prison there are real guys and jail house types, the difference being that real guys are hooked up out on the bricks,[12] while the others just say they're with a gang while they're in prison. You need to know gang laws and what's expected of you. Each Saturday on the yard we had a meeting to check out what was coming down. The shot caller was the main man who gave the orders, and I eventually reached that rank. We had various alerts we could signal through the grapevine, the most critical being a red alert, meaning our boys had to gather and move out—there was major trouble with rivals.

"We also had to keep our inventory and know who had the shanks,[13] TVs, cigarettes, jewelry, and zip guns. What we needed could either be brought in legit or by having officers smuggle it in for us, which they will do either out of fear for their safety and that of their family or for money. It didn't matter to us which it was as long as we got what we wanted.

"If an officer was killed, other officers came through the cell-blocks firing round after round in their rage. That got pretty scary. When one of our own guys messes up, he gets a V,[14] a five-minute beating by some of our biggest and strongest guys. It's not an experience I recommend."

8. Tell your background.
9. The general prison population.
10. Not affiliated with a gang.
11. A reputation for talking to the police.
12. Streets.
13. Knives.
14. A violation.

When Riko was released, he was pleased that his family had moved away from the old neighborhood to a new community—"so I could stay away from everybody and everything I knew from the past. But it's not that easy; the cops have computers, and they can know your whole history in a few seconds. In my new neighborhood they weren't about to leave me alone to see if I really was going to make it and do right. Whenever anything happened, mine was the first door they knocked on; I was guilty in their mind until I proved I was innocent."

Riko was picked up again in just that fashion. "But," he admitted, "one good thing *did* come out of it. The second time in I came to know the Lord. Earlier in prison I had wanted to quit all my gangbanging but couldn't. When I was back on the streets, I was determined to change and did to a large extent. Still, something was missing; I needed to turn good intentions into an entirely new way of living. But I couldn't do it on my own. Back in jail, I discovered that with Jesus in my life, I could change. Now I feel so much better about myself. I don't have to impress anyone or prove anything; I can make sensible plans for my future. Picking up a second birthday, a spiritual one, when I was 'born from above' like it says in the Bible in John 3, was the beginning of some very important changes."

One of those changes is being a positive role model to younger kids. "Now I'm reaching out to many of the young guys on the streets who know me and look up to me. I want them to know who and what made the difference in my life."

I was ready to testify for Riko at a sentencing hearing if needed, but he won the case and was reinstated on parole.

It's Not "When I Was Your Age . . ."

When kids seem to be spinning out of control, some parents try to regain their footing by recalling, "Back when I was your age . . ." But few, if any, contemporary adults *ever* lived in an age such as this. Not many of us grew up going to schools where violence was a fact of daily life and coke (the illegal drug) was easier to get than a Coke®.

The enormous changes that have created this different world did not happen overnight. By talking with parents about how it was when they were young, we see patterns of change emerging.

- First, kids lost their *innocence* when television became a staple in the home, presenting lifestyles that are alien and offensive to traditional families as normal and acceptable.
- Then kids lost their *respect* for social mores (beliefs, customs, traditions, manners) as the drug culture offered the challenge to "tune in, turn on, and drop out."
- Next, kids lost their *values* as intellectuals proclaimed, "God is dead," and everything sacred was up for grabs.
- Finally, kids have lost their *hope.* This is the first generation that does not see itself living better than its parents, a sure sign of the impact of world-wide economic and social upheaval. "So why get an education?" many young people ask. "Nobody's going anywhere." The key words for many urban kids in the nineties are *alone, fear, despair.*

Lacking a solid foundation at home, feeling helpless to change their situation, and without any higher purpose in life, too many youngsters can't see any reason for setting career goals or trying to accomplish more.

Many are *not* kids with a poor self-image. They may be very confident and self-assured, though often for the wrong reasons and over the wrong things. Some of them have all the ego of a successful entrepreneur in, say, junk bonds or a mismanaged savings and loan—and about the same ethical standards.

The road to jobs via education is a long-term affair, an alien concept to the urban kid's mind-set of instant gratification, a mentality fostered by TV, where everything happens in thirty-second time slots or half-hour segments and the good life happens effortlessly, as if by magic. And when the bubble is burst by nasty realities, such as the need for an education and the requirements for getting and holding a job, despair sets in for those who feel left behind in this media and computer age.

The family holds out some hope against the loss of innocence, respect, and values sucking the life out of our young people. And yet the American family is also in disarray. In the inner city, many kids come from homes where the level of family violence, marital discord, physical and sexual abuse, alcohol and drug abuse have reached such intolerable levels the kids flee to the streets in despair. And what do they find there? Gangs, petty crime, drug selling, and prostitution.

Over the past few decades our cities have turned back the hands on the clock of progress. The family, the church, the school, and the community have abdicated the hold they once had on youth and their standards of conduct. But vacuums don't last long and that's a major reason gangs have taken over. Unfortunately, in *this* different world, the kids are drawn directly into a lifestyle that, with incredible speed, can mangle and distort their emerging personalities, corrupt their moral values, and create vast distrust and self-hatred.

But this world, too, is included when John the apostle wrote, "For God so loved the world . . ."

Part 2

REASONS FOR HOPE

5

Three Ways Out

My experience with the kids on the streets convinces me that there are only three human accomplishments that guarantee escape from the urban jungle: completing high school; working consistently at a job; and getting and staying married. But it is precisely these three pillars of life—education, work, and marriage—that have collapsed among the underclass.

For instance, more than 25 percent of all students who start high school in Chicago will not graduate. What is worse, when we look at the blacks and Hispanics, the number of those not graduating rises to 50 percent. Many of those are the voluntary dropouts, but what is often overlooked is another tragedy: the "pushouts," kids forced out of school by a frightened and overwhelmed administration. After the age of sixteen, the State of Illinois does not require a student to be in school. This regulation originally designated how long officials had to pursue truant children. But now school officials have found it a convenient threshold for when they can *get rid of* unwanted kids.

I was sitting in a school counselor's office at one high school talking with a student who was having problems in school. I wanted to pull him away from his gang activities and help him see that education was going to be the key to his future. Just then the vice principal walked by and saw the kid in the office. He walked in and snarled, "I just checked your records; you'll be sixteen in three weeks. We can get rid of you on your sixteenth birthday, you know, and we will!" And he did.

Another Chicago high school principal, fed up with gang problems on his campus, told me he saw the answer as busing. He was not talking about a plan for integrating the races. What he meant was to put the kids on a bus in the morning and drive them around the city all day, never letting them off at any school—especially not his.

Of course, school administrators in many cities are over a barrel in their efforts to keep gang activity and violence out of the schools. But there are effective and proved alternatives to forcing kids out of school. I will discuss these later; at this point, however, it is important to note that the "solution" of kicking kids out into the streets does not help the teenager who is in trouble, it does not help the community, and ultimately it does not serve the school, either. It entrenches gangs ever more deeply in the community, and when that happens, they *will* make their way into the schools.

Out of the Trap

Since the options of escaping gangs through education, work, and marriage are not functionally available for many kids on the streets, the majority are destined for a violent death or a long prison term. It's just a matter of time. In my experience, there is only one other way to escape the trap: a genuine conversion to the Lord Jesus Christ. *Nothing* else provides any consistent hope.

For instance, Jimmy grew up in the Humboldt Park area and, with his brothers, was active in the Spanish Cobras. It was a life filled with danger in which he gave as good as he got in violent street wars. He was no stranger to the juvenile detention center and, later, the county jail. Busts come with the territory, but it shocked him when he was charged with murder; he didn't know how to deal with that.

Jimmy protested his innocence, but few believed him. An enemy was shot and police had an eyewitness, a friend of the victim who unhesitatingly identified Jimmy as the shooter. He was going to be put away for a long time. The police thought

Jimmy was long overdue for a conviction, and the opposition relished the thought of him behind bars—the longer the better.

In a cell block with little to do between long-delayed court dates, Jimmy started reading the Bible and attending chapel. What he read and heard appealed to him. Here was a challenge and—more important—a route to a better way of life, both here and in the hereafter. Out on the streets he thought God's last name must be "Damn"—the two words were used together so often—and "Jesus Christ" was what a person said when he hit his thumb with a hammer. But in jail he discovered a new reality, a genuine love, which God proved through Jesus' death for all the mixed-up guys on the streets, and Jimmy knew he was one of them.

When he read, "Believe in the Lord Jesus, and you will be saved" (Acts 16:31), that was as personal an invitation and opportunity for a new life as Jimmy could imagine. Jimmy believed and was born anew into God's family.

From that point on he had a new, positive approach to life, even in jail. He also had new resources to deal with all the agonizing delays and disappointments in court, as well as the boredom and pressures of life in a cell block.

He started to realize that if God could use someone like the apostle Paul to write some tremendous letters from a dungeon, perhaps God had a plan for *his* life too. He certainly saw little hope of his trial turning out well. Despite having fine legal counsel, an eyewitness made the state's case very strong. Though Jimmy prayed for God to bring out the truth, he really had no thought he could win. Even some of his own boys doubted his innocence. Certainly he could not expect a jury to view things favorably.

However, as the trial was about to start and while Jimmy was in a courthouse holding cell, the principal witness against him was also there, having picked up an unrelated case of his own. He wanted to talk to Jimmy, but Jimmy certainly was not anxious to exchange pleasantries with a young rival about to commit perjury in his trial. But he walked over and asked coolly, "What do you want?"

"Jimmy, I'm going into court and tell the truth. I didn't see you that day on the street when my homey was killed. I don't know who the gunman was, but I saw enough to know it wasn't you. I picked you out because I saw it as a good chance to get rid of an enemy, and the cops didn't care. They consider taking you out to be a public service," the youth explained to a thoroughly baffled Jimmy.

"But you've already given them a statement naming me," Jimmy replied. "If you change your story now, they'll get you for perjury, or they'll say my friends threatened you. Why are you doing this?"

"Whatever comes of it, I'll have to take the heat, but I don't think you'd understand if I told why I changed my mind."

"Why don't you try me?"

"OK. I've been here for a few months with my own case, and a chaplain has been talking to me. He gave me a Bible and talked to me about getting my life right with God, and I've done that. I got what they call 'saved,' and it means a lot of things are changing with me, one of them being I can't lie against you even though we've hated each other's guts out there on the streets. I guess the D.A. will get a surprise when he puts me on the stand."

A lying rival become a brother Christian? Jimmy was amazed at this turn of events.

The prosecutor certainly was shocked when a carefully laid case fell apart when the key witness said his earlier statements were not true. He assured the court that no one had threatened him or pressured him in jail or on the street; he had found God and wanted the truth to come out.

Jimmy was freed, and now as a community worker and leader he never forgets who changed his life and brought an enemy to his aid by convicting him to tell the truth. What is impossible in human terms is possible with God. As the old rhyme says,

> Humpty-Dumpty sat on a wall;
> Humpty-Dumpty had a great fall.
> All the king's horses and all the king's men
> Couldn't put Humpty-Dumpty together again.

But God can heal what all the magic available to modern society cannot.

The "Religious Option" Is All There Is

I spoke at a Chicago conference sponsored by law enforcement and neighborhood groups offering ways to deal with the gangs and was introduced by the words "Now we will have Mr. McLean discuss the religious option." That really got to me, so I grabbed the microphone and said, "We are not just another option; we are all there is!" What I meant was that unless God did a miracle in a kid's life, remaking him from the inside out, then every other community effort to solve the problems of youth violence was bound to fail. Education, family counseling, recreation, law enforcement, job training—all are good and important in their place but never a substitute for spiritual rebirth.

I told the law enforcement and neighborhood workers about the young man who was sent to a juvenile correctional center for a series of burglaries. He could hardly read or write, and the educational staff worked hard to catch him up with his class level back home. Then he was paroled only to return a few weeks later on a new charge: forgery. He was taught to read and write, but the spiritual emptiness and moral vacuum in his life was not addressed, so the person who was released was not a reformed citizen but an educated criminal.

"Or consider," I told my hearers, "the Chicago street youth who finally got his first job. I saw Coco after he got his initial paycheck and asked if he saved the money or helped his family or even put some money aside for the car he wanted. Each time he answered no. So I asked what he did with his money. Without a word he reached into his pocket and produced the .357 Magnum revolver he had purchased. A job certainly didn't solve his problem."

Some of the participants at the conference were offering creative, new recreation programs as *the* answer, so I noted, "Recreation centers can, if we are not careful, become gathering and recruiting places for the very gangs you want to stop. This is why our ministry aims directly at gang youth rather than operates a center. Of course, youth centers can be a real asset to a community, but they are not a magic cure-all."

I did not want to deprecate the value of all these services. They all have their place, but there is something more basic that *must* be addressed first in a troubled kid's life, and that is the matter of sin, salvation, and forgiveness.

CONFUSING SYMPTOMS WITH CAUSES

That is why, since 1949, my mission has been focused on introducing everybody I can to Jesus, especially young people in serious trouble. If success is finding out what God wants a person to do and doing it—and I am convinced there is no better definition of the word—then I am successful. To be on the cutting edge with front-line ministry and knowing so many young people who will never be the same once the Holy Spirit makes them children of God is the most rewarding experience imaginable.

Would I do some things differently? Of course. I look back with embarrassment at those times when I carelessly got in the way of the Spirit's working or when I blundered by taking things into my own hands. But would I change my calling or direction if I had it to do over? Never. A man or woman called to be a servant of Jesus Christ should never settle for lesser things like riches, fame, or power. To serve the Lord and to reach out to people is what matters.

Young people today need all the help they can get. Teenagers have never been angels, adolescence is often a troubled time of rebellion and rage, and today's crime wave flows across all economic and racial groups. But when secular analysts look at the problems, they tend to focus on *symptoms* rather than *causes*.

Listen to the observations of a group of counselors at a professional conference as they reported their research conclusions about today's youth:

- "The home, school, and church used to act as a restraint on youthful behavior. That doesn't seem to hold anymore."
- "There is usually just a mother alone raising a family. Even when there is both a mother and father, they usually work and are wrapped up in their own interests."
- "Some parents use drugs and alcohol themselves. The kids don't get the training and help they need to guide their behavior."

- "Parents attack each other physically as well as verbally and often do the same with their kids. And the kids in turn take their anger out on others."
- "There's no one for the kids to talk to, except the 'homeboys.' That's their family. They learn about sex together, use drugs together, and get their sense of belonging from the gang."
- "The only thing that matters is getting money and having things now. If big-shot brokers can take what they want—in the millions—then a kid is going to think he should grab the goodies he knows too."
- "Look at what kids see in the movies and on TV or listen to with their music. There is a steady diet of violence."
- "Heavy metal rock music constantly emphasizes sexual assault, bondage, and murder. When a kid listens to that day and night, he'll be influenced by what he hears."
- "Rap artists make violent and abusive conduct sound attractive. If guys listen to that day after day, they're going to think it's worth doing."

These professional counselors were describing what they consider the *causes* of a generation gone wild, while to me they indicated the *symptoms* of a spiritually dead generation in need of a resurrection, the new life Jesus Christ offers. Each of these symptoms represent serious problems, but their absence does not necessarily protect kids from the streets. Take the experience of Trigger and Fox, for example.

More Than Treating Symptoms

Trigger is not one of those neglected kids. His parents cared about him. They moved out of the city to get him away from the street gang wars. But after only a short time in the suburbs, they found that the gangs had followed them. And Trigger, their youngest son, was an eager recruit to the Two-Six Nation that had branched out into the suburbs.

He did not get arrested for anything serious—mainly a few disorderlies with station adjustments—and was released to his parents. He is a smart kid, not only in terms of the streets but in his schoolwork too. He looks younger than his sixteen years and is a fastidious dresser and a real hit with the young ladies.

And he had an innocent smile that caused most unsuspecting adults to think him the nicest of boys. But they should have looked twice. He wasn't.

Trigger was totally loyal to his gang, and, bright as he is, he carried a good deal of influence in the group. His specialty was how to do things without getting caught. He modeled that role every day at his high school, where weary officials often knew what he was up to but could not seem to nail him. Search his locker, there was nothing to find. Get word of a gang plot, Trigger knew nothing. Some trouble breaks out in the hallways, Trigger was there but just didn't see anything.

"Yeah, they do have a problem, don't they," he said when I asked him about it. He did not want to get kicked out of school, and his goal is to be the first person in his family to graduate. At the time he planned a career in the military with a college education provided by Uncle Sam.

"You're going to join the Marines on *our* side?" I once asked.

"I think so—at least for now." He grinned.

Trigger's gang chief supported his good goals by telling him, "Stay in school, do your work, get good grades. If anything serious happens at school, you stay out of it. You just can't get kicked out."

He followed that advice, usually. But he hated to miss a good fight with its chance to smash the rivals and impress the girls. And the girls do tend to admire guys who are daring and adventurous. Trigger certainly did not want to disappoint them.

The boys often joked with Trigger about his appeal to the ladies, despite his small size. "Be careful, they may rape you," he was warned by one.

"You can't rape a volunteer," he replied.

His gang chief introduced me to Trigger on the streets and told me, "Now here is a challenge for you. See what you can do with *him.*"

If I had to take on the reformation of Trigger by only dealing with the symptoms of his situation, I would have been smart to quit right there. But when the Lord starts working on a person, even a street gang kid, things can get more interesting than any of us plan.

THE SEARCH FOR TRUTH

Hid well behind the smooth front Trigger gave the world was a searching, eager young man really wanting to know what life was all about and what really mattered. Anxious to reach Trigger was a Savior who died on a cross to give him a life far beyond the next party or gang war. My assignment from the Lord: bring him in.

That took some time, prayer, and careful effort. We had some good discussions, but the real issues were not the questions about whether the Bible is true or if there really is a God. Those often are just smoke screens. The real question is, Does the person want to change? Anyone who really wants to do what is right and seeks to find it, will soon know what is true (John 7:17).

But before Trigger could know the truth, he had to let me get to know the real kid behind the front, and there was much there for which he needed forgiveness. Finally he opened his life to the Lord, and it was a beautiful experience. Trigger now regularly attends my home church and actively reaches out to help the kids he knows. Of course, many people didn't really think he'd changed when he was still part of the Two-Six Nation, but he has changed, and he enjoys watching others try to catch up and figure it all out.

Among Trigger's enemies was Fox, a member of a rival gang. Fox figured that his street rep would get a major boost by taking Trigger out of the box.[1] Fox took his boys to the local McDonald's where Trigger worked and stationed some at the front door and some at the back while he went in with a gun tucked in his belt.

"Where is Peter?" he asked, referring to Trigger by his real name.

"He's not in today; he's sick," said the clerk.

Fox left deflated. He had planned to take Trigger out right there in McDonald's. It would have been a big-time move. The letdown was heavy, but Fox resolved to get Trigger some other day, and he was not going to let this go for nothing; he'd call

---

1. To kill him.

Trigger and put some fear in him by telling him how close he had come to dying.

That evening when he got Trigger on the phone, Fox threatened him in the usual crude language of the street. But Trigger did not respond in kind. He did not even hang up; he just listened.

When Fox was through, Trigger calmly asked, "What do you get out of all this?"

Fox responded with more abuse, but Trigger just said, "What's wrong, man? Why are you talking like this? You sound real uptight."

MALICE DEFUSED

That was hardly the reaction Fox expected, and it caught him off guard. Before he realized it, the two of them were into a discussion about their lives and where they were headed. Trigger told about his goal to be the first member of his family to finish high school, to go on to college, and later his intention to serve as a Christian youth counselor. Fox was amazed. But there was more to come.

"We ought to get together and talk about this!" Trigger suggested.

"We can't meet," Fox replied. "If I arrange it, you'll think it's a setup, and if you arrange it, I'll be sure your boys will hit on me. No way."

"Well, I'll tell you what," said Trigger, "there's a man I know; he's like a reverend. What if he arranges for us to get together? You'd trust a minister, wouldn't you?"

Fox did not know what to say. Though he had been raised with a church background, he had no idea how to understand this plan. It could be a real set up. On the other hand, he was very curious.

"I'll tell you what," said Trigger, "*you* call him and set it up. That way you'll know I'm not trying to trap you"—which is why I got this unusual call from a street youth I had never met or heard of asking to arrange a meeting.

It took a great deal of careful maneuvering to get the two guys together, but they finally spent an afternoon talking and actually got along remarkably well. They recalled some of their street war battles from opposite sides as well as dating experiences with young ladies they both knew.

A few weeks later the three of us met again, and this time the talk centered on the Lord's power to destroy hate and bring enemies together, not only with each other but with Him. Fox knew the teachings of the Bible well; he had grown up with it in his home and church, and it was still with him, no matter how hard he tried as a teenager to put it out of his life.

That evening Fox prayed to accept the Lord and the following Sunday joined Trigger at church, where Trigger introduced a new believer to the people he had enlisted to pray for Fox. They often attended church together, changed from enemies to friends and now brothers in Christ.

Beyond Our Control . . .

But such changes do not come automatically. Parents can agonize over the direction of their wayward son or daughter for years with no positive response. But while such kids may get beyond the *control* of their parents, they are not beyond the reach of their prayers. Through much heartbreak, often expressed during sleepless nights by a pillow stained with tears, the answer seems so long in coming as the rebellious child continues to charge headlong toward self-destruction.

Jerry's mother was a parent who walked this path. She is a deeply spiritual, praying woman, and when she came home from her work as a medical professional, it was most often to attend church or seek the Lord on behalf of her son. When the answer eventually came, it was in an unusual way that she would never have imagined.

Jerry was nervous and for good reason. The young man standing a few feet away in the alley had a shotgun pointed at him. Jerry was armed with a .38 special aimed at his opponent. The other youth had the advantage in fire power. Jerry could shoot first and thought he might have to, so he looked straight into the eyes of his rival, not daring to blink or look away. Neither antagonist moved. Neither spoke. Both were sweating.

Suddenly a police car turned into the alley, and both boys instantly ran. The one with the shotgun was quickly captured—

his weapon was too big to stash. But Jerry knew his escape route. He dropped his gun in some bushes along with his gloves. Then he quickly ran through a gangway to the street beyond, calmed himself, and walked casually with other kids heading home after classes. A police car soon rolled up to the curb beside him. The officers got out.

"Assume the position," barked the cop.

"Who, me?" Jerry answered. "I'm just walking home from school. Check me out," he offered, as he spread-eagled with his hands up against the wall.

The officers questioned him briefly; they were impressed by his polite responses and particularly his neat appearance. There was no insolence in his speech, no gang colors on his clothing, and he was not wearing baggy pants or any other standard gear of a street gang youth. The officers let him go and continued on with what would be a futile search for the gun-toting youth.

It had been a close call, but it was neither the first nor the last time a nice appearance and a pleasant smile kept Jerry out of the clutches of the law. In the few times he had been picked up, he had used a false name and address so that, when he was released for a later hearing, that was the last officials saw of him.

Intelligent, personable, and neat almost to a fault, Jerry is a Colombian youth who lives in a nice neighborhood. Yet he was an Imperial Gangster known as "Gato G." And Jerry is not a minor player in anything he does. He was zealous, "down for the nation," as the boys describe it, a leader among his peers, always thinking and getting away with nearly all he did.

Smooth at school, slick on the streets—the good, respectable youth to one group of people and the calculating street gang leader to another crowd—Jerry seemed to have everything under control. Well, almost everything.

. . . BUT NEVER BEYOND THE POWER OF PRAYER

There was his mother, her prayers, and the prayers of her friends at church. She had never let up on Jerry, insisting that he go to church with her and reading daily from the Bible to him. Even though he was persistent in his rebellion, she did not give up. The two were well matched. She did not know all of her son's involvements, but she knew he was a long way from the Lord. Still she believed God would one day answer her prayers to bring Jerry to Himself.

One day things began to change for Jerry. His close friend Julio was arrested and charged in the stabbing death of a youth on a city bus. At the juvenile detention center Julio was held for adult court trial. But while there he heard the Word of God, not at the family breakfast table as Jerry did but from a black youth held on an equally serious charge. That boy—only fifteen—used an unusual degree of wisdom and patience in leading Julio to the Lord. Later, Julio asked me to contact his good friend Jerry out on the streets, and I agreed to make the call.

The timing was right; things were not going well for Jerry. There were bitter street encounters with rivals that left both physical and psychological scars. He was frustrated, angry, pressured, and he didn't know whether he should get a piece[2] and take out some of the opposition or just end his own life. In the midst of his total confusion he finally did something he usually only pretended to do to placate his mother—he talked frankly to the Lord.

"If You're really there," he almost screamed, "and You care what happens to guys like me, if anything can really change, then send someone to tell me. Because if You don't, God, it's all over."

AN OPPORTUNE CALL

A few minutes later his phone rang. I had no way of knowing how opportune my call was, but I told the stunned young man on the other end of the line that I was a minister, wanted to talk to him about the Lord, and was sent by Julio—about the last person Jerry would anticipate caring about the Bible or its message.

Jerry didn't need to hear anymore. God had answered his prayer, and he was not about to let his opportunity pass. This time the tenor of his prayer changed: "God, You know how I can fake people, con them, get what I want. You know what I am on the streets, not the nice guy adults think I am. You know

2. A gun.

it all, and I want You to change it—change me—forgive me
—let me start a new life. I want to be on Your team—to help Julio
and the other guys before they get where Julio is. I've got a long
way to go, Lord, but let's You and me get started."

The next day as Jerry and I met, he eagerly accepted the Bible that Julio had asked me to give him and told me what the
Lord had started in his life. Jerry is growing in his commitment
of faith, reaching out to a rather amazed group of friends, and attending college. He is married and active in his church youth program. A mother's faithful prayers are being answered.

One example of how Jerry has changed is seen by his influence on Pucho. Pucho's career on the streets began at age
twelve when he was busted selling drugs with his father (who
later went to prison on a murder conviction). Pucho fell into
the gang lifestyle and quickly learned his way around. He and
Jerry were gang partners, so it was no small surprise to Pucho
when Jerry came to know the Lord and started changing.

Pucho's curiosity was aroused, and one Sunday he joined
Jerry and me at church. Later, we talked together about his
own life, and he took the same step of faith that had made such
a difference in his friend. Pucho's own young brother had no
use for gangbanging but was into satanic worship and rituals.
He could not believe it when Pucho chilled out and started
reading a Bible. Eventually Pucho was able to bring his brother to know the Lord too, and the pair make an outstanding
young witnessing team now. Pucho is working, finishing
school, and eagerly reaches out to share the good news with his
friends *and* former enemies. His "raps" highlighting the change
in his life have been a special feature at many church gatherings. His ambition: to be a police officer.

But Can There Ever Be *Peace* on the Streets?

My staff and I are not social workers with Bibles under our
arms, though that may be a valid calling for some; rather, we
are evangelists who care for the whole person. We are not on
dangerous streets to make bad men good, though that may be a
result, but rather to make dead men alive. "Because of his great
love for us, God, who is rich in mercy, made us alive in Christ
even when we were dead in transgressions" (Ephesians 2:4).

In truth, we may never stop all the dope dealing and gang wars, any more than we can use a cup to empty the ocean. But we can see progress, lives being changed, and caring people making a difference.

I know veteran leaders of street gangs who—acting on their new faith in the Lord—will take whatever risks are necessary to help others, reach out to their former enemies, and work for peace. Guys like Flaco, J. R., Rico, Kojo, Dr. J., Joel, Miguel, Carlos, Chente, Lionel, Bandit, Jorge, Oreo, Carl, and Sal—they all say, "Just tell me what to do, where to be, who to meet, and I'll be there. And don't worry about the danger; I've lived with that all my life, so now I might as well put my life on the line for the Lord and His cause." They know their way around on the streets, but they have also found the way to the Savior. And He is still changing lives; the miracles have not stopped.

The cry of the streets is for peace. It will come only when the Prince of Peace reigns and rules in each heart and life. The cry of the hurting for Him is one we can no longer ignore.

6

Paths to Peace

The car advanced slowly. It was dark, and the street lights highlighted not only the vehicle but its careful route down the center of the one-way residential street. A casual observer would conclude that no one was around to notice, but in the narrow gangways between the houses more than a dozen pairs of youthful eyes kept careful watch on the unfamiliar intruder.

Two boys were in the car, and their slow pace was deliberate, the first indication that they wanted no trouble. The all-too-common drive-by shootings are most frequently done from a car that races down a street and stops by a target at the curb. The gunman fires and then speeds off. The boys in the gangways understood that scenario all too well, so the peaceful intent of the approaching car and whoever was in it was not lost on its intended audience.

Still, they did not recognize the car and could not see who was inside, though eventually the street lights outlined a driver and a front-seat passenger. The car came to a stop in the middle of a block on South Drake Street, at that time the heart of Villa Lobos territory. The Villa Lobos (literally the Village Wolves) were a small but closely knit group of Mexican-American youth on the southwest side of Chicago.

Lobos suddenly appeared from everywhere, darting out from between houses and parked cars to surround the strang-

87

ers stopped in the middle of their neighborhood. Several of those young men had their hands on their guns, ready for instant response. The windows of the car lowered, and the boys outside gasped in amazement; there sat Roberto and Eddy, two of their worst enemies and the last men they would ever expect to see in their hood.

The boys in the car spoke first. "We're not armed. You can check that."

"You better believe we will," replied the closest Lobo. "In the meantime, just sit there and don't move." The firmness with which he gave his command left no doubt that he would respond at the slightest suspicious movement.

"What do you want?"

"We need to talk to Mr. Kent right away," Roberto answered just as firmly. Kent was the street name of the 30th Street Lobos leader, and he was in his house nearby. One of the boys ran to alert him to the strange occurrence, but surprisingly when he came out he walked directly to the car surrounded by his boys.

"Stand back," Kent ordered his boys. "What in the world are you guys doing here?" he asked in amazement when the other Lobos were out of earshot.

"We came to warn you," Eddy replied. "Our boys are planning a hit on your street tonight. We met earlier over in our territory," he added, nodding in the easterly direction from which they had come. "They're mad over somethin' and decided tonight was the time to settle it. We asked them to hold on while we got our guns. It gave us just enough time to come over here and tell you."

"If you don't want to see anybody hurt," Roberto added, "have your boys stand back, stay off the street. Maybe we can get through the evening without anyone getting taken out. At least it's worth a try."

There was not much time for debate, but as Roberto and Eddy revved their engine to take off, they said to Kent, "We'll see you at the meeting Sunday." And then the car sped away.

"What was that all about?" asked the Lobos as they gathered around.

"I haven't got time to tell you now, but I want everybody off the street. Their boys are going to be over here right away to pull a hit, but we won't be around. They won't find a target, and believe me they'll be looking. Stand back between the houses and at the attic windows. But they are not to know we are here, and most important there is to be no shooting."

"Why not?" one boy challenged. "We could take 'em by surprise and turn this into a real shooting gallery!"

"Sure," Kent shouted back, "and then they'll know we're here, jump out of their cars, and we end up getting guys on both sides hit, not to mention our houses and families. Use your head! No action! Tonight we take a pass."

That's how a kid gets to be a leader on the street—using his smarts, not just muscle or guns. Kent is a natural leader, intelligent, articulate, and quite ready to take command.

His plan went off without a hitch. The rivals came twenty minutes later from all directions and raced up and down the street looking for Lobos to take out, but they might as well have stayed home. There wasn't a Lobo in sight, not a target to be found. In disappointment and anger their enemies finally sped off; a few rounds were fired in the air in frustration, but no one was hit. A well-planned raid ended up a total bust. Back in their territory no one sounded more disappointed than Roberto and Eddy—such was the role they had to play with their peers.

DO THE RIGHT THING

Later I asked Roberto and Eddy why they had taken such a risk. "Those guys haven't been your friends in the past."

"No big deal," Roberto said. "It just seemed like the right thing to do."

"Look," I persisted, "you guys could have been killed out there. I certainly don't want you taking risks like that."

"You didn't ask us to do it," Eddy replied. "We've taken chances a lot scarier than that and for things not nearly as good. We were trying to keep some guys from getting hurt, so we figured, why not?"

That daring action to prevent a massacre was not as spontaneous as it appeared. The young men from rival gangs, Mr. Kent, Roberto, and Eddy, were well acquainted—and not just from the streets where their groups warred.

It began when some of my friends in the Boulevard Latin Kings asked if I knew their allies, Mr. Kent and the Villa Lobos. I did not, so they offered to take me and Rod den Dulk, a visiting California psychologist, to meet the new group. That has been one of our best ways to get acquainted on the streets, just as in the business world or anywhere else: the right person making an introduction can often guarantee instant acceptance. The other successful method we have employed is to make contacts at either the juvenile detention center or the youth section of the county jail with follow-up or home visits that put us in touch with their peers. By either method, who you know and who introduces you are all-important when you are on the street.

Mr. Kent was more than a little amazed to have his King friends introduce him to a minister and even more stunned when I gave him and each of his boys a *Living Bible.* (It is a bit of comic relief in my life to watch those kids looking fierce on the street corner holding a Bible. But they usually manage.)

Mr. Kent remembers how he felt with a Bible in his hand: "I ditched it back in my house as quick as I could—bad for the image, you know. Funny thing, though, I never forgot where I put it, and a few days later when I was feeling really down I got it out and started reading. Amazing stuff in there, and it got me · thinking."

SLOW PROGRESS

There were some interesting discussions with Kent and his boys over the next few months as to just what the Lord was saying to them in terms of a commitment of faith and changes in lifestyle and attitude.

Some of those sessions were blunt. My message: "Are you guys going to follow the way things are done on the street or the way Jesus taught? You can't do both."

Kent and I also talked about his enemies in general and Roberto and Eddy in particular. When I first mentioned the pair, the response was quick: "I hate 'em." Then he ran down a lengthy list of insults and hurts he credited to them and their boys.

I did not dispute the facts he laid out. I just asked, "Haven't you done just as much back to them?" He shrugged, then admitted that was true. "Have you forgiven them?" I asked.

"Never! They and all their boys can rot in hell as far as I'm concerned."

I let the angry remark go, but when I was getting ready to break up our session, Kent asked, "Aren't we going to pray like we usually do?"

"No," I replied, "it won't do any good. As long as you hate someone else, there's no point in your asking the Lord to forgive or bless you." Then we took a look at some pointed references in the Bible.

"Here, Kent, check this out," I insisted. "Love your enemies and pray for those who persecute you" (Matthew 5:43), and, "Forgive us our debts as we also have forgiven our debtors" (Matthew 6:12), and, "Do not repay evil with evil or insult with insult, but with blessing" (1 Peter 3:9). Pretty heavy stuff for a person carrying a load of anger.

"If you want the Lord to forgive you, then you've got to forgive those who've wronged you. That's God's idea, not mine. So if you have a problem with it, take it up with Him."

I asked Kent what he wanted in life, and he said, "A family, a good job, some peace and safety on the streets." Not bad goals.

"And don't Roberto and Eddy want the same things?" I inquired. He agreed they probably did.

The Father Fathers Brothers

Next came the clincher. "Kent, if God is your Father now that you've been born anew into His family, and if those rivals also have received Him, then what are guys with the same Father?"

"Brothers," he replied, quickly getting the point.

"Even if they're rivals?" I pressed. Again he agreed. "Then shouldn't brothers at least respect each other?"

Somewhat hesitantly he nodded. "And I bet you've got a verse on that, too, haven't you?"

"Yes. It says, 'When a man's ways are pleasing to the Lord, he makes even his enemies to be at peace with him'" (Prov. 16:7).

"Let me read that myself," Kent asserted, and we spent some time discussing it. It does not say enemies will all become close pals, but it does say they can respect each other if their relationship with the Lord is right. However novel such an idea was to a street youth, Kent saw that it made sense.

I ended our discussion by suggesting a meeting with Roberto so they could talk together, and I offered to hold it in neutral territory where they would both feel safe. Shortly afterward I had the same conversation with Roberto, and the meeting was arranged.

A United Nations

We met in a restaurant, and at first the pair was very ill at ease, but gradually they relaxed as they shared notes on common goals for their boys and their futures. Deep down both were sick of the wars and the hatred and wanted something better in life, but so far they had not found a way out. They began to talk about how to go about finding it. Ninety minutes later they were more like long-lost friends reminiscing than rival gunmen.

I suggested we meet again and that each of them bring a buddy to the next meeting. They agreed, and the second session went as well as the first one. Gradually the sessions grew until today it is a regular meeting called the United Nations. The name comes from the fact that each group attending is considered a "nation." More than forty representatives from twenty-some Chicago street gangs and organizations have attended the sessions, currently being held at Calvary Memorial Church in Oak Park. It is an honor to be invited, and there are some careful ground rules:

- Only guys who are invited can come.
- The group has a veto over any new attendees proposed.
- If anyone feels that tensions are too high for a certain mix, we do not try it.

• Our ministry volunteers pick up the guys and bring them to the meeting and take them home so that no one has to walk through enemy territory.

• No colors, guns, or drugs are allowed.

Many of the young men are professing Christians. Others are not, but all are in sympathy with the aims of the meetings.

The guys at our meeting are all leaders whether or not they have a title. "There are three types of guys on the street," Mr. Kent once said. "Guys who make things happen, guys who wait to see what's going to happen, and guy's who don't know what's happening. This is the first group." We sometimes invite guests to our meetings. In addition to many media reporters and prominent church leaders, we once welcomed an F.B.I. agent with a fascinating report on his life and work. Of course, our kids were very attentive!

The meeting opens as each street kid and staff person introduces himself, and then we are quickly into the discussion of the evening. There are no ice-breakers or entertaining features such as are mandatory when suburban church youth groups meet. Urban gang kids see death around them every day and are so busy dodging heaven or hell that they do not need to be enticed into facing reality.

There are often tensions in the room, a natural result of bringing long-standing enemies together. The atmosphere can be unusually heavy if there has been a recent incident on the street between the represented gangs. The worst that has ever happened were a few shoves between boys, always quickly stopped by the rest, who insist that the potential combatants respect the nature of the meeting, much as they would a church service.

Actually, there was one fight. It occurred outside the steak house where the group ate. Kenny, an African-American Vice Lord, ran across one of his high school teachers, also black, drunk, and beating up a white man in the parking lot. Kenny stepped in to help the white man. The teacher was furious and told Kenny, "You can't do that; I'll get you back." But Kenny reminded his teacher that they were not in school, and he could and would stop the fight.

We regularly discuss matters affecting the crisis areas of their lives. Sometimes we discuss their rights and responsibilities when they encounter the police. At the United Nations' meeting and in other sessions with individual gangs, attorneys such as Clarence Burch volunteer to advise the kids. Clarence is a prominent African-American Christian layman who sees representing his clients in a private criminal defense practice as a vital part of his service to the Lord. He tells the members of his attentive audience that they should not get smart with police on the street or lie, but also they should insist on their right to remain silent when arrested until they talk to an attorney. Some youths in the group will display an "Officially Retired Gang Member" card we issue with photo, name, and address. It often causes a stir when used as identification on the street.

LESSONS TO LEARN

The heart of the evening discussions is aimed at applying the message of the Bible to the kids' lives and teaching them responsibility, respect, and caring for others. One lesson started with reviewing the story Jesus told about a man who was beaten and robbed and the various people who passed him by until finally the despised Samaritan intervened (Luke 10).

"Who did you guys identify with most as I read that account?" I asked.

They laughed. "The robbers," said several.

"Look, Rev," suggested one young man, his face scarred from street battles, "you want us to be good. But remember, it's your job; you get paid to be good."

"Does that mean you're good for nothing?" I replied. Again some smiled. But we looked carefully into Jesus' account and saw the religious man who passed by not wanting to be bothered and the Temple lawyer who would not intervene unless he could get a paying client. We discussed the innkeeper, who did the job he was hired for, and of course the Samaritan, who proved by his care and kindness that he was a neighbor to the victim.

As they reacted to the story, one boy pointed out, "That's what Jesus did for us—went way out of His way to give us a break." Several in the group nodded in agreement as another boy frankly admitted that he might stop and even help a stranger, but he would really have a struggle if he recognized the victim as an opponent.

"Maybe one reason those other guys split was if they stayed around the cops might think they did it and start asking a lot of questions," suggested one kid.

"But that's where we're supposed to be different if we're lined up with the Lord," another interjected. "Any of us would help a homey in trouble, but it really takes being tight with God to want to help a guy from the other side. You aren't some square or phony if you feel sorry and help someone; that's cool, man."

VALUES

Another night we talked about what is right and wrong in their world. "Well it sure ain't the same as with your crowd, Rev," one guy volunteered as the discussion started. Then they listed the rules of the street:

- No one snitches to the Man.
- We don't get mad; we get even.
- Nothing is wrong if you aren't caught.
- If it feels good, do it.
- If you can make a lot of money doing it, it must be right.

I challenged those values head-on, reminding my hearers that Paul said we should not "conform any longer to the pattern of this world" (Romans 12:2), and, "There is a way that seems right to a man, but in the end it leads to death" (Proverbs 14:12).

Sometimes we discuss popularity, reputation, and character—words they have never bothered to define and tend to think of as synonymous. Of course, they're not, so we work through the differences: "*Popularity* is what you think you are; *reputation* is what everybody else thinks you are; but *character* is what God knows you are."

I stress absolutes in right and wrong, keeping and respecting the law, personal responsibility, and caring for others. This concern comes out in another area when we talk about their girlfriends. Many in the group simply view girls in terms of physical attraction and their availability to fulfill the guys' desire for pleasure. When I point them to God's standards, it is as if I had brought a message from an alien planet.

Once a boy said, "That reads pretty good, all about love being patient and kind. Did Shakespeare write that?"

"How would you know?" another boy quickly challenged as the crowd laughed.

They settled back, and I reminded them that *people* are to be loved and *things* used, not the other way around. People are important to God, and they should be important to us—which rules out premarital sex, abortion on demand, and anything else that demeans people and lessens respect for life.

The guys of the United Nations readily agree that one reason people lack respect for others, their rights, and their property is because they lack respect for themselves. Many of them have been put down for so long by adults that they have come to believe they are worthless— until they find the confidence that comes from being a child of God. Respecting themselves is basic to their respect for anybody or anything else.

"At our school they have condoms available at the health center, and they teach you in class how to use them," one kid volunteered while we talked about not taking sexual advantage of others.

"That's about the moral equivalent of showing you how to rob a bank and get away with it," I replied, creating an uproar of diverse opinions on how to deal with teenage temptations, sexual pressures, and the threat of AIDS—all relevant to deciding how they show respect and care for their girlfriends. The answers don't come easy.

But I keep coming back to the importance of people over things. People are to be loved and cared for, a view that challenges every basic tenet of selfishness and criminal activity in which these young men have been involved since their preteen years.

THE GOSPEL MESSAGE

"But what happens when we blow it?" one guy anxiously asked.

"O-Z," a Chicago gang member, armed, on a dangerous street. . .

and later, with his Bible.

Mayor Richard Daly, center, with Miguel Ramirez, left, a former street gang member, and the author at Chicago Rotary Club #1.

Volunteer Mark Beedle, second from left, who ministers with three young inmates in the school wing of the Cook County Jail.

Tony and Freeman, right, welcome a suburban high school student to Vice Lord Village—called The Holy City by that organization—in Chicago.

The author, second from right, on the street with Boogie Cool, Chuy, and Wino of the Latin Kings organization, with their emblem in the background.

Mark Beedle, fifth from left, with a group of young Latin Kings on a camping trip.

Shorty B., left, and Little Buff, both of the Bishops, with weapons, on a Pilsen area street, Chicago.

Adam Salas, left, the author, Wayne Shepherd of Moody Radio, and Brian "Little B" Davis. Salas and Davis were street rivals who came to know the Lord and later were introduced to each other on Moody Radio's program "Prime Time America."

Dr. Arthur DeKruyter, pastor of Christ Church in Oak Brook, Illinois, welcomes three young Chicago street veterans to his church.

Robert, a leader of the Bishops, and his brother Tony, with their ladies on the Chicago street.

Freeman of the Vice Lords organization, known as Princen Baby, proudly displays his hat and shirt.

A young member of the Latin Jivers gang on Chicago streets.
(Photo by Bob Coomb)

Jessie, second from left, and Carlos, right, of the Imperial Gangsters, during a special presentation of the YFC ministry at Wheaton College.

Members of the Two-Six gang on Chicago streets.
(Photo by Bob Coomb)

A Chicago street gang member shows his gentler side with his young son.

Scone, of the Renegade Vice Lords, at the Henry Horner Homes housing project in Chicago.

Freddie, a street gang member, with his motorcycle and gun and gang sign.

Demetrius, right, who at eighteen was the youngest inmate on death row in the Illinois prison system, and Curtis, left, his cousin, serving a life sentence.

Chicago street gang member.
(Photo by Stuart-Rogers-Reilly, Copyright ©1990)

The author, left, and Tom Locke, right, of Youth For Christ in Chicago, with street gang youth in the background.
(Photo by Stuart-Rodgers-Reilly, Copyright © 1990)

"When you've done wrong, you need to get forgiveness from the Lord, and that's available when you tell Him you're sorry and really mean it," I responded as I showed them 1 John 1:9. "Then you must do everything you can to make right the wrong you have done. Whether you win or lose your case at court, and whether or not the judge orders restitution, *you* do whatever is possible to make it right."

"You mean God will forgive all the crazy stuff I've done?" asked another dubiously.

"Sure, just tell Him the truth," one guy suggested. Some have genuinely understood the message. "You ain't gonna shock God; He already knows all the stuff you did. So it ain't no surprise to Him."

"How about this," I interjected, "God will forgive our sins but not our stupidity." There were blank looks.

"I get it!" someone said. "God forgives us for sinning against Him, but if we do something dumb, we'll have to face the consequences, like at court, or even with scars on our body."

My staff and I try to help them understand how victims feel who have been hurt, robbed, or had a loved one killed. A number of our boys have been through those experiences themselves and recall vividly the physical and emotional pain they or their family suffered when they were attacked or a brother was killed. It is important for these boys to understand that people are angry when they have been violated, and they will want to strike back, sometimes physically but most certainly through the courts. Most innocent victims are not big on forgiveness but want judicial revenge—heavy, hard, and long. Our guys have seen that.

At the end of the session comes a prayer time like few church people have ever experienced. We get requests like these: "Pray for Willie from our gang; he was shot last week and is in serious condition. He might not make it, so pray for his O.G.,[1] his lady, and his sister who are really hurting."

Only a few minutes later another guy requests prayer for Jack. "He's one of my boys. He's in jail charged with shooting Willie." And we remember both.

1. Mother.

Admittedly the sessions caused a certain consternation in my apartment building where they were held until we outgrew the available space. There was enough media attention that my neighbors knew what the group was about and frequently asked, "Is this the night your friends are coming over?" When I indicated that it was, they often responded, "Good, we're going out!"

Fortunately the group has never been a problem to the tenants or at the steak house where we meet for dinner after each meeting. When the manager first asked one youth what the group was, he was met with a serious look and the reply, "You really wouldn't want to know!" The manager did find out, though. Media attention has answered his query, but he considered this the best youth group of any community or church organization he serves.

A key factor is the changing faces at the meetings. The original boys are long gone and no longer attend, their places taken by a new generation of younger brothers.

Blood Thicker Than "Colors"

Changes do not always come as fast as I would like to see them; there are those who fall back, and there are many kids on the street we do not have the resources to help, or for their own reasons they refuse our ministry. But through all the crises, it is wonderful to see God's faithfulness.

Even when violence continues to swirl around our guys, God's hand of redemption can still be seen as He builds bridges of friendship and understanding between some very unlikely subjects. Right before our eyes we can see that unity through the blood of Jesus Christ is thicker than the gang loyalty that separates guys on the streets.

Angel, for instance, grew up on the streets and was stealing cars long before he could apply for a driver's license. At thirteen he was a gang hit man, wise in the ways of the streets if not school. He was eventually sent to the Illinois Youth Center at St. Charles. There his curiosity about our group sessions and the chaplains' program was aroused by another resident who met the Lord and exhibited some remarkable changes. In time, Angel also accepted the Lord and began looking forward to returning home and getting his life together.

Some time after his release, he and his brother were walking near their home on a rainy Sunday evening when three youths stopped and offered them a ride in their car. They were rivals. Angel and his brother were reluctant to accept the offer, but the driver said, "Don't worry, it's raining out; we'll give you a lift wherever you're going." So they climbed in the back seat and drove a mile away to their destination. The conversation was easy and pleasant and the brothers thanked the driver for the ride as he pulled over to the curb to let them out.

Suddenly the driver shouted a gang slogan as he pulled out a gun and began firing. Angel's brother was hit in the back, and Angel took three bullets at close range in the face, shattering his jaw. Still he did not fall but grabbed for the door handle. The driver jumped out, shoved Angel to the ground, got back in the car, and sped off.

Angel's brother died in his arms on the street as the wailing siren of an ambulance was heard heading for the scene. Angel was in critical, painful condition, and his survival was doubtful.

At the hospital there was another concern: with the media reports on the tragedy, the gunman or someone else might come to the hospital to finish the job so that there would be no witness in case of an arrest and a trial. Security staff and police put a special guard around Angel and made sure no one with street ties, especially not a Latin King, got near the intensive care unit.

A few days later a young man did show up asking to see Angel, and he was dressed in the colors of Angel's assailants. Security staff were immediately alerted, and they carefully questioned the would-be visitor.

"Angel and I are friends, and I came to see him," Shy explained, making no attempt to hide his colors or the symbol on his jacket. "Ask Angel."

When Angel learned that it was Shy downstairs, he immediately requested that the visitor be brought up, and the security people obliged. Angel and Shy were friends; they had met at our United Nations' meetings and had been in a number of church programs together. Angel was confident that what united them as believers in the Lord was far more vital than the street rivalry that separated them.

Angel could hardly talk; his jaw was wired shut following extensive and painful reconstructive surgery. But he could write on a slate and was elated to see his friend. I soon joined them, and there were tears in all our eyes as we saw Angel's suffering, and Shy observed for himself the extent of the injuries for which his boys on the street were responsible.

A few months earlier Shy would have been the last person to care about anyone else, certainly not a rival. He was making too much money and having too much fun to be concerned about anyone else. Unusually intelligent and perceptive, he knew all his gang's leaders in his area, and they in turn marked him as a comer. At age fourteen he picked up a sideline with some older friends: stealing cars in Chicago and trading them with partners stealing other luxury cars in California. This activity was far removed from the usual evening joy-ride in a quickly snatched car most street kids settled for; Shy was "in business."

He might have stayed in business for a long time and climbed the ranks of the organization except for a problem. Though everything seemed under control, he was still restless, looking for answers about his future. He was searching for something more but didn't know what it was and certainly not where to find it.

A gang member from Shy's section introduced him to me. "Shy is a guy who is really an influence in our whole area. He's young, but he's got smarts, and I think you'll like him." He was right, and Shy and I had some good talks over several months that centered on the things in life that are really important, especially what the Bible says.

Then one of Shy's school friends invited him to an outdoor rally in Humboldt Park to hear David Wilkerson, the New York preacher and author of *The Cross and the Switchblade*. Having been fascinated by both the book and the movie, Shy went. As Wilkerson spoke, Shy did some serious thinking about his life and where he was headed. At the invitation he went forward, prayed with Wilkerson, and made a public profession of faith in the Lord.

He was excited as he told me of the experience, and his conversion produced some external changes in his life. Soon he was earning straight A's in school, and the following year he became class president. He got a job earning considerably less than he had made with the stolen cars, but this was honest money. Shy also became active in our United Nations meetings as a means of influencing his friends and even reaching out to former rivals. One of those opponents was Angel, with whom he developed an especially close friendship.

Thus, while police were making sure no rival got near Angel in the hospital, they freely admitted Shy practically every day. He came with a Bible in his hand, not a gun. To the surprised nurses Angel and Shy showed a compelling Bible verse, "If anyone is in Christ, he is a new creation; the old has gone, the new has come!" (2 Corinthians 5:17). And with this pair the old hatred had indeed dissolved, and a new brotherhood had come.

Part 3

BARRIERS TO SUCCESS

7

Doing the Right Thing . . . Isn't Easy

Jesus never said His way would be easy. "Sit down and count the cost before you sign on with Me," He warned, "to see whether you will be able to complete the task."[1]

Young people on the street who respond to the gospel are often faced with the high cost of turning their lives around. As the gang members in the United Nations are realizing, God forgives our sins and wipes the slate clean, but the consequences of our sins still have to be faced. That was true for Danny, someone I met in a correctional institution in California before I moved to Chicago.

A PH.D. FROM SWU

Danny's boys should never have messed with him. He had a good memory and a sharp mind. When he shook your hand firmly, you felt that with very little effort your hand could be crushed. Yet there was a calmness about him—no need to make a big impression or put on a display of power. He knew who he was and what he could do.

I first met Danny ("Cat" they called him on the streets) when he was sixteen years old. While his mental and physical powers were still maturing, this Mexican-American youth was

1. Paraphrased from Luke 14:25-35.

already a person to be reckoned with among his peers. Growing up in the barrio of east San José in central California, he was a veteran of the streets long before he graduated from junior high school. He did what he had to do to survive—stole, fought, warred with rivals—and for pleasure smoked some marijuana and made it with the ladies. He had a Ph.D. from SWU: a Pimping and Hustling Degree from Street-Wise University.

It was all but inevitable that he would end up in jail—the only question was at what age and which one. He was fortunate; he was still a juvenile when the court-ordered commitment was to the William F. James Ranch at Morgan Hill, California, a good facility with strong emphasis on education and counseling. Danny was well liked by the other wards (which was not surprising) but also by the staff (which was). He treated the teachers and counselors with respect, worked hard, did well in school, and showed encouraging indications of being successful when he was released back to the community.

On Friday nights a team of volunteers and I spent the evening at the ranch, leading a discussion group in the dining hall and spending time on the grounds counseling informally with the one hundred young men in their midteens. The openness of the staff and the relaxed atmosphere of the ranch lent itself to giving us ministry opportunities. We made friends with the wards and introduced them to an experience of faith in the Lord. During the fifteen years of my ministry there, my colleagues and I saw the lives of many young men changed for a lifetime.

Danny was our friend. He came to the meetings regularly and often invited other Latinos to come with him. He read the Bible and enjoyed discussing how its truths related to life today. It was that connection between the message of the Bible and its demands on his life that presented Danny with a real conflict. And it was his difficulty in resolving that issue that kept him from making a public commitment of faith, even though he remained our good friend and supporter.

When we were alone he would say, "I know I can open my life to the Lord and He will accept me, but I also know there are steps to following Him I'd have to take to be genuine in my faith. I couldn't go to church on Sunday and praise the Lord, and then spend the rest of the week on the Devil's payroll, selling drugs and warring on the streets. It'd have to be one or the other."

I could not have said it any clearer. He understood the choice. I showed him where the Bible (quoting Jesus) said the same thing: "If anyone would come after me, he must deny himself and take up his cross and follow me" (Matthew 16:24). There was clearly a price to identifying with the Lord. To tell these young ranch men anything else was to allow them to build on a shaky spiritual foundation, like the man in one of Jesus' parables who built a house on sinking sand. We dared not suggest that being a Christian would solve all their problems or help them with their case or gain them an early release. The gospel message is not a quick fix or another temporary emotional high. It's a new life we receive from above (John 3). And attitudes and conduct change *after* a person meets Christ (2 Corinthians 5:17; Philippians 1:6).

Accepting the Lord put Danny on a collision course with his gang lifestyle on the streets. His was a long and rough journey before a major crisis brought him to the point of making a break with his old ways. But when the change did come, the impact was enormous.

When Danny was released he made it a point to keep in contact with me. The path of his life and our relationship was a rocky one because he was still without a strong base to his faith by which he could handle the pressures and temptations that surrounded him. The result: Danny was soon lured back into more serious criminal activity.

Yet there was another side to him: his love for Maria. His girlfriend, by no definition a gang girl, was not only beautiful and intelligent but had high moral standards. In fact, after I got to know her, I could not imagine why she stayed with Danny. But she did, and eventually they married and had two beautiful daughters. Danny was a proud father and insisted I come over to their apartment and take pictures of the babies. He wanted the girls to know me as an uncle—quite a compliment to an Anglo.

THE GULF WIDENS

But the fine family and friendly contacts could not hide Danny's drift away from what was good and right. "Cat's" abilities were recognized by one of the most powerful gangs in California, the Nuestra Familia. He quickly rose through the ranks to become a key lieutenant, with assignments in drug trafficking and prostitution as far away as Fresno.

Our conversations became more infrequent and strained; we agreed on little and had little to talk about. I reminded him of his family, and he answered angrily, "I'm doing it all for them, so they'll have good things and a nice home. Don't worry; someday I'm going to quit."

"Danny, remember what we said at the ranch meetings: it's never right to do wrong to get a chance to do right. You'll always plan to quit. There's going to be just one more big job, just a little more money to make, or another score to settle. But you're going to end up dead or in jail. Then what will happen to your family?"

I felt the strain of our troubled friendship. I liked Danny but hated what he did. Many times I just wanted to give up and forget him, but somehow the Lord would not let me. Like a loving parent, whose prayers follow a wayward son through grief and heartbreak, I was not going to let go. I believed that some day the Lord was going to break through Danny's stubborn, proud will and claim that young man for Himself.

Then Danny was arrested, charged with armed robbery and home invasion. He was looking at a twenty-eight-year prison sentence. A distraught Maria called me with the news and asked me to go see Danny.

Danny's bail was set at $100,000, and he had no way to make it. When we talked in the jail counseling room, he was adamant: "I had nothing to do with that robbery and what happened at the house. I was home with Maria at the time; you can ask her."

"That may be true," I replied. "But nobody is going to believe your wife in the courtroom. I don't think she'd lie for you, but the jury doesn't know that."

"My boys will clear me," he insisted. "They'll get me a good lawyer, arrange the bail, and then help me get the guys who did this to admit it so I'm cleared."

I had no such hope and told him so. He would be on his own, and the boys would let him go down. They may be "friends to the end," but it's amazing how quickly the end comes when a guy picks up a big case.

I was right. The weeks wore on and still no help—no bail, no lawyer, no anything. Danny went on trial and was convicted with two other gang members on all counts. He was just a few weeks away from being sentenced to prison for a long time.

Finally he understood and was enraged. "The boys aren't going to do anything! They let me down. They've messed over the wrong man once too often." But even Danny realized his chances for revenge were slim. "It'll have to wait—maybe till I'm on the yard at Q.²"

Not necessarily. If he *really* wanted to get back at the gang and do it the right way, there was one other route open. Danny took it, and California gang power has never been the same since.

UNDERCOVER

A few weeks later the boys in the Nuestra Familia were surprised to see Danny out. "Got out on bond," he explained. "My sentencing hearing got delayed for awhile." They didn't ask why sentencing was delayed or where the money came from, assuming his family had somehow arranged his release. They should have asked. They were so confident of his ties to them that none of the gang voiced any suspicions at Danny's sudden good fortune.

Besides, Danny's muscle and brains were sorely needed on the streets. The rival Mexican Mafia was pushing up north from Monterey Park and creating problems for the N.F., so Danny was welcomed back into the inner circle, where he was quickly involved in weapons supplying, drug deals, prostitution, and other criminal activities. He was made lieutenant with the promise of higher rank to come.

2. San Quentin Prison.

Late one night he called my home, verified that I was alone, and asked if he could come over. "Of course," I said.

When he arrived a short time later, he sat down exhausted. "I had no idea how hard this was going to be," he said, shaking his head slowly. "I just came from a meeting where large quantities of cocaine and heroin were distributed for suppliers on the street." He opened his jacket to reveal a hidden tape recorder. "I've got it all on here."

"Take it easy and be careful," I cautioned. "There's a lot more of this ahead."

Danny had agreed to be an undercover informant for the Federal Bureau of Investigation. His assignment was to go to the top of the gang, getting full details of all their activities for later indictments by the grand jury.

Hidden cameras often recorded his street contacts. A seemingly innocent old panel truck parked by a meeting site actually held video and sound equipment with infra-red film and other devices to fully document all of Danny's contacts. His family did not know what he was doing lest a careless word slip out in innocent conversation in front of the wrong people. His life was literally on the line.

TURNING THE CORNER

The pressure was enormous. Danny often came by my apartment late in the evening just to unwind and talk. After he debriefed me about that evening's crisis, talk turned to other things, including the Lord, whom he had accepted at the ranch several years earlier but with whom he struggled over the direction his life should take.

Now older, more mature, thoroughly disillusioned with gang life and all it stood for, with a family to care for and his life in danger, Danny was no longer dodging the call of God's Spirit in his life. He knew what it meant. This time he was open, responsive, and walking closer with the Lord. And although Maria could not at first share in the secret of his F.B.I. work, she did become his partner in building a Christian marriage and family.

It would have been strangely out of character if he went to a church in his neighborhood, but he could come to the church

I attended in the suburbs without arousing suspicion. Danny and his family came as often as possible.

Then one night we faced another crisis.

"I just got back from a meeting with the guys and José was there," Danny said. "The cops picked him up later on some old charge, and he's in jail. He's a good guy, really; he doesn't belong in this mess. But he's in it now; we've got him on tape. There was nothing I could say when he showed up, no way to warn him. He's going down with the rest of the guys when this is over." There were tears in his eyes. The only other time I saw him so emotional was when he talked about the effect of his life on Maria and his girls.

After holding his head in his hands for a few minutes, he looked up at me. "You've got to go and see José. He knows you and trusts you. You've got to tell him exactly what I'm doing for the feds and ask him to do the same thing—join me. That's his only way out."

"It's not that simple, Danny," I said. "Are we sure the feds want him?"

"They'll be glad to take him if he knows what the deal is and wants to join. Besides, I've already mentioned it to Agent White, and he says we can try."

"But, Danny, suppose I do what you ask. I ask José and then he's not interested. All he needs to do is break the news to the gang and you're a dead man. That's a terrible risk."

"Just do it!" Danny said.

A BIG RISK

The next evening I sat across the desk in the jail counseling room confronting a young man with news he would find hard to believe. José listened without a hint of expression as I told him his best friend was not only a federal informant but had built up a case against him. Now he was being asked to be part of the plan himself. When I was through, José buried his head in his hands and said nothing for several minutes. Finally he spoke.

"I thought Danny was up to something, getting out of his case like he did and back on the streets. I even thought he made a deal, perhaps working for the local cops, but I never imagined it was for the feds." He spoke carefully, slowly, weighing every word.

"I can't go with him. When this is over, he's going to have to move away and never see his friends again. I can't do that. No way."

He paused, noticing the concerned look on my face. "I know what you're wondering, Rev. Now that I know the truth, is Danny safe? Yes, he is. I'll say nothing. He'll have to come to court and testify against me along with all the rest, and I'll go to prison. But that's the end of the road I'm on; it's too late to change now." José was quiet for a moment. "In a strange way, I'm glad Danny's doing this. I wish I had the guts to do it, too. He's my friend, even now. And I won't betray him."

I breathed an audible sigh of relief.

José smiled, breaking the tension. "That wasn't easy for you, was it?"

I shook my head.

"Let me tell you, you should have got to me before the gang did," he went on. "But maybe it's not too late. Leave me a Bible, and let me catch up on it." He was right; it wasn't too late for his heart to change, but by every practical measure José's life was ruined, and I felt very sad as I left.

Danny knew how, if not when, his unique undercover work would end. One day he came by to see me. "It's tonight," he said simply.

Both of us knew what he meant. A moving van would drive up to his house and load all the family's possessions. Maria would finally know the full details of all she must have suspected about her husband's adventure. The family would get in cars with U.S. Marshals and simply disappear without a trace. They would be moved to another part of the country, perhaps hundreds of miles away. When they moved into a new home it would be with a new name and full identification, an employment and credit history on file, and a waiting job. This was the federal witness protection program.

Danny would return to the Bay Area to testify at the trial of his former street partners who were about to be arrested. In a short time all those arrested would know the identity of the informant who had so carefully built the case against them, but by then he would have disappeared from the community where he had been raised.

For his parents and other close family members the separation would be hard. Contact with Danny and Maria would only be by mail directed to and from U.S. Marshals. Danny's response to correspondance would give no hint of his new identity or locale. Periodic secret meetings would be arranged at still another location under the watchful eye of Danny's protectors. There could never be normal family interaction, trips home for the holidays, even a phone call on an impulse. Every contact would be carefully screened and planned. Danny's life and the lives of his family were at stake; so was the outcome of ninety-two federal trials soon to begin.

As we talked, we both knew that this would be our last visit and that Danny would be leaving in a few hours.

"Shall I contact you when we get settled?" he asked, even though he already knew the answer.

"No," I told him sadly. "As much as I'd like that, you shouldn't. I know too many of the young men in this case and others still out on the street. I have to be able to tell them honestly that I don't know your whereabouts or what has happened to you. I just pray that wherever you settle down you will meet with some good Christian people, put this life behind you, and go on with your family to serve the Lord."

We prayed together, shook hands firmly, and then Danny turned and walked out of my home and my life.

Danny did his job well. His testimony was key to convicting all the gang leadership and severely damaging their whole operation. In fact, federal informants have been so effective that the Nuestra Familia is said to have killed fifty of their own members they suspected of being informants. Danny has not been one of them, but I have not seen him since our farewell in San José. If he should read these pages, he will know he has not been forgotten and that a friend still prays for him.

TRUTH OR CONSEQUENCES?

If I can help a young person who is in trouble with the law but is responding to our ministry, I will go to court, indicate our interest in him, and testify to the progress we have seen. I will not do this, however, when he wants to take the stand in court and lie about his guilt. But sometimes the choices kids have to make are not simply black and white.

I met one young man who had been arrested for several robberies. Jesse insisted that he was innocent, even though two victims picked him out of a line-up. The boy insisted that he was at work or at home with his family during the times in question. But as confinement wore on him, he decided to make the best deal he could with the state's attorney. He asked if I would come to court with him.

"But you've insisted all along you're not guilty!" I protested. "Now, just to settle the case, you're going to tell the judge you did the crimes? I can't support you saying you did the robberies if you didn't."

Jesse looked away. "Tell me," he asked, "if I didn't do them, who looks enough like me for witnesses to pick me out instead?"

That was easy. His brother, just a few years older, was very much like Jesse in appearance.

"Right. He's already in a lot of trouble, serving heavy time. If he gets these charges added on, he'll never get out of the joint. I can't let that happen. My family doesn't want that to happen. I'll only get a short sentence, so I'll take the fall for my brother. Guess that's what brothers are for!"

His attorney had a hard time understanding, too. She believed they could establish with good witnesses where the young defendant was at the time of the crimes, but he would have none of it. He pled guilty to crimes of which he was innocent to help his brother. Was he right? Was he wrong? All I know is, he was thinking of someone besides himself. But it was a sad day in court.

Pay Now or Pay Later

On the other hand, Patrick *was* guilty. He had been heavily into drug dealing, clearing several thousand dollars a week by moving dope for a sales ring. At age seventeen, he was on his way to prison on a selling charge, but his boys offered help (something they talk about more than they actually do): "We'll bail you out to wait trial, and we'll get you a good lawyer."

But Patrick did not see it that way. He explained his feelings to Tom Locke (of our staff) and me in one of our jail counseling sessions.

"Look, I'm getting my life straightened out. I've come to know the Lord here, and I'm serious about serving Him. I want to get my life together and do some good things. Sure, my boys will get me out and pay the legal bill, but then they'll hand me a supply of coke, tell me to sell it, and give them back their out-of-pocket expenses. And I'll be right back in a business I want to be done with." Patrick set his jaw. "So I'm staying in jail. The court will give me a public defender, and I'll probably go down to the joint and serve time. But at least I'll be my own man, and when I get out I'll owe nothin' to nobody on the street."

Patrick looked at Tom, then at me. "That's what the Lord wants me to do, and that's what it's going to be."

Facing Down the Jail Deck

Sweet Pea, an African-American youth active in the Spanish Cobras on Chicago's Near North side, was a natural leader. With a world of opportunities at his fingertips, he chose instead to direct his talents to the streets, with its excitement and fast money.

Late one night Sweet Pea and his brother came home to find a drunk acquaintance of their mother's attacking her. The enraged brothers killed the man, and it wasn't long before murder charges were filed against the boys and their mother. Released on bail, Sweet Pea wanted his mother to have the best attorney possible. So he took part in an armed robbery to get money to help her and was caught. He was quickly back in the slammer on new charges with a bail set so high he would not get out again.

Inside he came to youth services regularly and became a good friend to our ministry team. He was straightforward, helpful, and honest—qualities in short supply around a jail— and quite open about wanting to find something better than what the street offered, even with all his power and rank. Anything Sweet Pea did, good or bad, he did with all his energy and ability. When he eventually gave his life to the Lord it was not a temporary escape. He meant to be as true a follower of Jesus as he could be, even in jail, no matter what it might cost.

And it did cost him.

A young kid named Drac came on the deck, strictly neutron[3] and unfamiliar with the power structure among the inmates. The first day he sat at a table reserved for the leaders of the various Folks gangs. One angry youth was about to attack Drac when Sweet Pea signaled him to chill out. Sweet Pea decided to simply talk to the new boy later and set him straight. But then Drac accidentally spilled some milk, and it got on the clothing of the boy who was already furious. Again Sweet Pea stepped in to keep the situation from exploding.

That night the Folks groups called a meeting on the wing; they were angry. This new kid deserved to be beat up because he sat at the wrong table and spilled the milk. Furthermore, the group decided that because Sweet Pea had helped the kid, he would be the one assigned to carry out the mission.

"Get serious," Sweet Pea said. "The kid is new here; he didn't know where to go at lunch. I'll tell him and take care of it. As for the milk, the kid was nervous; it was an accident. You can't give the kid a violation[4] for that."

But the boys did not agree, and the more they argued the angrier they got. Finally they decided that if Sweet Pea would not give the boy a violation, then *he* would get a beating himself.

"Then go ahead and give me the V, because I'm not touching that kid," he said. And he submitted to a beating that left him bruised and sore for several days.

The next morning Sweet Pea was still in his bed feeling every blow from the attack when one of his partners came in. "Are you getting up?" his friend asked.

"Who wants to know?" grumbled Sweet Pea, wanting nothing more than to sleep in and to be left alone.

"The guys out there are taking bets on how many days it will be before you get up and go back to the jail school."

---

3. Not affiliated with any gang.
4. A beating for breaking gang rules or for disrespect.

Sweet Pea had handed the boys one victory the previous evening; they weren't going to get another. They could knock him down, but he would not let them think they could keep him there.

"All right, help me up," said Sweet Pea, painfully throwing one leg and then the other off his bunk.

Later that day I saw him walking stiffly down a jail corridor.

"What happened?"

"Nothing serious. Just a heavy workout; got to learn to pace myself better." And he walked on. It was several days before I learned what really happened, and it was one of the other boys who told me.

He did well in the school program and was featured in special stories on jail education in both major Chicago daily papers. After the incident with Drac, respect for him among his peers was even greater, and he often brought most of the wing to our youth services. One kid who came to know the Lord before he was released was Drac, and nobody was happier than Sweet Pea.

BETWEEN LIFE AND DEATH

Among Sweet Pea's friends on the deck was John. In gang terms they were bitter rivals, but as Christians active in the chapel ministry they were good friends. But Sweet Pea's partners did not agree, especially since John was charged with killing one of their friends. Making matters worse was the mysterious appearance on the jail deck of some police photos of the victim in John's case taken after the shooting. They showed the deceased youth in full color, covered with blood. The victim's friends were enraged, even though many of them were charged with similar offenses.

Once again the Folks called a meeting, and Sweet Pea was on the spot. The group wanted John hit[5] in the jail and would settle for nothing less. Being outnumbered twenty to one did not deter Sweet Pea in the slightest from expressing his opinion.

"Who set you guys up as judge and jury? Most of us here have murder cases of our own. Leave him alone!" he shouted

5. Killed.

defiantly, scaring the lookouts who stood on the deck watching for any approaching jail officers.

But the boys would not budge. John was to die. Finally Sweet Pea saw there was no way he could change their minds. "OK, you win," he said softly. "John gets hit."

The group murmured their assent, glad to see Sweet Pea had finally come around to their way of thinking.

"But there's just one thing," he continued.

"What's that?"

"Before you kill John, you'll have to kill me." Sweet Pea made the statement calmly. But it was so outlandish they could not believe it.

"You heard me. Before anyone takes on John, you'll have to take me out first. Now let me leave while you guys talk this over and decide who gets the honor." And he walked out.

The meeting broke up quickly in confusion. No one was going to take on Sweet Pea, certainly not kill him, one of the highest ranking, most respected boys on the streets and in the jail.

Several of the boys from the group stopped by Sweet Pea's cell later. "Why did you do that? You were taking a terrible risk."

"It wasn't a risk; I meant it. And I did it because what divides John and me on the street isn't nearly as important as what unites us as brothers in Christ."

It was Sweet Pea's strength of character and commitment that influenced many young men on the deck to turn to the Lord. They in turn reached out to others, and that influence continued long after Sweet Pea was transferred off the wing.

Danny, Jesse, Patrick, Sweet Pea—each one is a reminder to me that taking up our crosses to follow Jesus is just the beginning of the journey. But for these youth, who have often lived a lifetime on the streets before age twenty, there are other barriers to be overcome, some of their own making and some not.

8

The Hard Edge of "Justice"

In spite of the many young people who are turned around by Jesus Christ, and in spite of reconciliation between street enemies through our United Nations meetings, significant barriers to broader change remain. These barriers sabotage peace efforts at every level and keep some kids—however genuine their personal conversion—from escaping the tragedies of the streets.

Unfortunately, one barrier to peace can be the police. All too often they do not behave in ways that elicit respect from the young people they are trying to control. The nationwide broadcast of the incident on March 3, 1991, in which police officers were videotaped beating a motorist in Los Angeles, was exceptionally brutal. The victim, who was clubbed more than fifty times, stomped on, and shocked with a stun gun, suffered skull fractures in nine places along with numerous other injuries.

However, that kind of brutality is not unique. In that instance the public outcry led to a nationwide Justice Department investigation of police brutality complaints. The Justice Department receives an average of 2,500 criminal civil rights complaints each year, about 90 percent of which relate to misconduct by police officials. But of those, only 2 percent are prosecuted because police misconduct is so difficult to prove.[1]

1. Justice Department Spokeswoman Amy Casner, quoted in "L.A. Police Beating Prompts U.S. Study of Brutality Complaints," *Chicago Tribune*, 15 March 1991, p. 8.

Not Always "Officer Friendly"

But there are other ways the police waste their respect. For instance, it is common for the police to pick up a kid for "questioning," drive him around, and then let him off in a rival gang's neighborhood. Technically, the police have not committed an offense, but they know what they are doing: the kid's life is in danger. Another common trick in Chicago is to confiscate a kid's colors. Police will demand that a kid take off his jacket or shoes with identifying colored shoelaces. Then the police will drive off and sometimes give the jacket to a rival gang in exchange for a gun or information. I have no interest in defending gang colors or insignia—we do not allow them in our United Nations' meetings—but on the other hand, there's nothing *illegal* about wearing a black jacket with a beige, green, or gold stripe down the sleeve.

I know that there are times when the police need to use force, but anytime they use force and do not make an arrest, there's a good reason to question, Was the force necessary, or were the police the offenders?

Take the case of Crazy J. One night two Chicago police officers stopped him and several friends—boys and girls—and ordered him to turn a Los Angeles Kings hockey team T-shirt inside out. The officers felt it promoted the Latin Kings and was therefore "illegal." Crazy J complied. But then the officer wanted him to do the same with his sweatpants marked with the same team insignia. Crazy J refused. The officers put him in the car and drove him to a deserted area, where one of them beat him badly.

He was next taken to the police station, where the desk sergeant ordered the officers to take him to a hospital emergency room for treatment. When he was returned to the police station, no charges were filed and he was released. A few hours later I saw him, his clothing covered with blood, his face and body a mass of cuts and bruises. I took him to the police Office of Professional Standards, which investigates allegations of brutality by officers, and Crazy J filed a complaint. A police photographer took pictures of his clothing, but later the department reported both the pictures and negatives missing from their files. Fortunately I had taken similar pictures and gave them copies of mine. But, as with most cases, there was no follow-up to what was a clear and documented case of brutality.

When I get frustrated at seeing sloppy police work, actual dishonesty and brutality, and defendants treated with contempt, I try to remember that every day police officers risk their lives on the streets as walking targets. Then they come to court and are questioned by lawyers and judges, who make much more money than they do, most of whom have never entered a dope house or stopped a suspect not knowing whether he might pull a gun or sue for illegal arrest. Realizing that the job is high-stress helps keep the problem in perspective. And of course many police do not behave in an unprofessional and counterproductive manner. But this is still a major problem on the streets as we try to encourage young people to have respect for the law and law officers.

LAWS THAT DO NOT HELP

Sometimes doing what is best for kids who get into trouble is thwarted at higher levels. The story of Steve demonstrates this problem.

Steve's parents, Eric and Anne, were not the usual dysfunctional or high-risk parents I encounter with children in trouble. Of Swedish descent, they lived in a nice part of the city, where Eric was a fire department veteran and his wife a travel agency representative.

I met them at their church after speaking at an evening service. They took me aside, anxious to share their experience.

"Our son Steve was in junior high school when we became concerned about some disturbing patterns," Anne volunteered. "He was a good student, but then he started cutting classes, his grades dropped, and he lost interest in sports and most other activities. We were concerned about some of the friends he was running around with: drop-outs, partying kids, and generally kids from less stable homes than ours.

"We should have recognized these indications as more than boredom at school," Anne admitted. "He was actually running with a drug-using crowd, but we couldn't bring ourselves to believe our son would ever get involved."

A high school counselor eventually alerted them that their son had a serious problem. The school had found some marijuana on him at school and suspended him. The parents arranged to see a substance abuse specialist, and the sessions with all three of them went well for a while. "Steve thought we were too strict and wanted his freedom," Eric said. "We said we were anxious to hold the line in our home because we believed our standards were right." Eric and Anne thought they came out of the meetings understanding each other better.

"But our problems were not over. In fact, they got worse. Steve was picked up by the police for theft and sent to the juvenile detention center. He was released to us, and immediately we went to see our pastor as a family to talk through what was happening. Steve listened politely, but there was no change.

"We tried so hard to make things come together," Anne said. "Both my husband and I work, but we made sure we had time with Steve. We went to sporting events as a family, took a nice vacation to Disney World, and allowed Steve to bring along one of his friends for companionship. We're not negligent parents; we aren't all wrapped up in just getting material things. We're like many families, working hard to make ends meet and provide for our children some of the good things we didn't have when we were growing up."

"I'll never forget the phone call I got in the early hours of the morning from the district police station," Eric said soberly. "They were holding our son and two other boys on a robbery charge. I hurriedly dressed and drove over to the station. I've lived in this area a long time and have worked alongside many of those police officers; I know them well. At the station I found a sergeant who was a friend, and he said I could see my son alone in an interrogation room. He assured me no one would listen to our conversation; it would just be between father and son."

When Steve came in, the first thing Eric asked him was, "What happened?" He told his father that he and the other two boys had been driving around in his friend's car, and they stopped at an all-night convenience store. The driver said he was going to buy some cigarettes and be right out. Soon he came running out, jumped in the car, and took off in a hurry.

Steve asked him what the rush was, and the boy admitted that he had robbed the store. Just about that time a police car with lights blazing and siren screaming pulled up behind them, and the three were arrested on robbery charges.

"At first I was angry that Steve had been with guys who would do anything so crazy," said Eric, "but if his story was true, *he* hadn't really done anything wrong. Nonetheless, I wanted him to learn a lesson, so I decided not to post bail for a while. However, I did tell him I would call an attorney and have him come over to the station. I also told Steve to tell the officers anything they wanted to know; the truth could only help him."

In the few days he was in jail, however, Steve was brutally beaten by other inmates because he was not in one of their gangs and would not give them any of the food he had bought at the jail commissary. "So much for leaving him in jail to learn a lesson," Eric said painfully.

"But there was worse to come. Steve was charged with armed robbery even though only one of the trio had entered the store and confronted the clerk, who told detectives she saw two youths in the car outside waiting. My lawyer explained that in this state and many others there is a *law of accountability* that makes everyone legally and equally answerable for the crimes of anyone in a group if they failed to try to prevent it. We don't have an accomplice law; everybody is equally guilty. A lot of naive kids like Steve get badly hurt by that. Still our lawyer agreed we should fight the case and perhaps convince a jury Steve really didn't know what his friend was going to do."

At the trial some months later Eric was in for another surprise. The prosecutor introduced as part of their case against Steve a recording of Eric talking to his son at the station that evening. Right at the start of the tape the jury heard him ask if anyone would listen and the sergeant assured him their visit would be private. But it made no difference that the sergeant had lied; the tape was still admitted as evidence.

"I had advised Steve to tell the truth, thinking it could only help him. But in the eyes of the prosecutor, all Steve had to do was admit that he was *in* the car and *at* the store and he was guilty—on the basis of the accountability law. I know now

I should have told him to say nothing until our lawyer had an opportunity to talk with him and be present for any questioning. I would never have told Steve to lie, but I wish I had told him not to answer questions until he talked with a lawyer."

Steve also gave detectives a statement, which they typed up and he signed, that was quite different from what he had told his lawyer and his father. When Eric asked him about it, Steve said, "If detectives want you to make a statement and sign it, they have very effective ways of getting a suspect to 'volunteer' it."

All three youths were found guilty of armed robbery and were given a mandatory prison sentence. "We couldn't believe this was happening—not to us, not to Steve!" Eric said. "If he had done wrong, then he should pay for it, but all they wanted to do at court was throw these kids in prison. It didn't make sense."

"The laws are tough on kids these days," I agreed, "but perhaps you can appeal the case and get a new trial. It sounds as if there are some good questions for a higher court to consider."

"No, there won't be an appeal," Anne replied sadly. "Let us finish. Steve went to prison where he was like a fish out of water. The first week he was there, he was gang-raped by other inmates and was so ashamed he didn't want to even tell us, the chaplain, or anyone else what happened. But the torture of it all got to him. His letters home and phone calls to us were cries of anguish."

"But why not an appeal?" I persisted.

"Steve took it out of our hands," Eric finally answered after a painful pause. "A few months ago he tied a sheet around his neck and jumped off the top bunk in his cell. They found his body at the next roll call."

COURTS CAN RUN AMUCK

Not all situations are as tragic as Steve's, but many kids get caught in a court system that seems to obstruct justice as often as serve it.

Garry was charged with armed robbery in a case where two youths had robbed a man at gunpoint of his wallet, credit cards, and expensive jewelry. Garry had a long history of run-ins with the juvenile court and had finally arrived at the age where his offenses could be dealt with in adult court, a transition the police had long awaited.

Garry's jury was typical, perhaps a little better than most. The state's case opened with the victim describing the suspect, Garry. Nonetheless, the victim admitted that in the dark he had not gotten a good look. Then how had he picked out the accused? Investigating officers "helped" him with a photo book at the station, and when the page with Garry's picture came up, they prompted him by saying, "That must be him. He's a bad guy. He's your man." The victim agreed, and Garry was soon arrested.

At the station Garry was advised of his right to remain silent and have a lawyer present for questioning, but then that right was quickly forgotten. One officer kept threatening to grab Garry by the throat and smash him up against the wall. The other officer had to "calm him down"—a common *good cop/bad cop* routine. When the bully left, the friendly officer offered to give Garry a break if only he would admit, not to the crime, but "just say you were there, and we'll let you go." Garry agreed and even signed a paper with that admission on it. They had him! He did not have to commit a robbery to be guilty; with the accountability law, just being there was enough. He was charged.

These techniques show why two common elements of a trial should be viewed with a great deal of skepticism: eyewitness identifications and confessions. Eyewitnesses can be honestly mistaken or deliberately intent on setting up a street enemy by naming him as the offender, whether he is guilty or not. As for confessions, if a police officer wants a statement from an accused, more than likely he will get it. The bruises will disappear long before the case comes to court, and if getting rough does not get the information, being sympathetic probably will. In either case, truth ends up being a casualty.

There was an unusual confession obtained by police from fifteen Vietnamese youths charged with robbing business owners from their homeland and some houses of prostitution. The police held a line-up for the youths involved without attorneys, but the victims were confused and unclear in both their language and identifications. So an alert officer had victims and accused change places, then asked the youths to look at their supposed victims under the line-up spotlights and pick out those they had robbed. Only one youth, the youngest of the group, realized the legal danger he was in and declined to answer. The rest readily identified their victims and only then contacted attorneys.

It works on the other side, too. A witness may truthfully testify against a defendant and then—fearing retaliation—come in for the defense at a post-trial hearing to say he was mistaken or forced by police to testify. The jury probably will not believe the change of heart, but it could help the witness's life expectancy on the streets, where fingering a gang member does nothing for one's health.

A caring judge has to balance society's interests against a defendant's right to be presumed innocent and have a fair trial, but that can be frustrated by a police officer's illegal search, brutality to a defendant, and even perjury on the witness stand. Some cops simply want to pile up convictions like so many notches on a belt, and there are prosecutors willing to do the same thing.

When Garry's trial was due to start, the defense asked for a postponement because they needed to contact a "Mr. Green" first. I had never heard that name mentioned, but a lawyer quietly told me that meant they had not got all their money from Garry's family and the case could not proceed until they were paid. The judge readily understood and granted the delay.

Garry's defense was that he was with a particular young man named Alan at the time of the crime, and they were partying with some friends, several of whom I brought to court to testify as to his whereabouts. So why had Garry been arrested? It was a pattern that operates wholesale within the criminal justice system: the police are under community pressure to get somebody for a crime, and often they are not overly particular who is charged. More than a few officers have explained this casualness to me: "If he didn't do this one, he probably pulled other jobs where he didn't get caught, or he'll do one next week. So why sweat over whether he really did this one? Let's just take him out now." This week's victim will probably be next week's accused in another case; that's life in the big city.

Garry's case involved an uncertain identification and a dubious confession on the state's side versus alibi witnesses who were friends of the accused. After an emotionally stirring oratory by the opposing attorneys, each appealing for justice, the jury went out to decide the case. Four hours later the verdict was in: not guilty.

I expected Garry to be released. But, instead, the judge, who wasn't pleased with the verdict, dismissed the jurors and announced, "You may have put it over on that jury, but you can't get by me." He then ordered Garry held in custody for probation violation. His reasoning: If Garry had been with Alan—his alibi—then he was in the company of a known felon and had broken his own probation. "Lock him up."

This was no ordinary judge. A feisty young boxer in college who came up from the streets and worked his way through school, he prided himself on being unorthodox. He had the right political connections, so nobody interfered with what he did. That included sending one street kid to the mental hospital for ten days because "If I sent you to jail, you'd brag about it; now I want to see you tell your boys you were in the funny farm!"

JUSTICE DELAYED IS JUSTICE DENIED

Another casualty to justice is the expectation of a prompt trial. With street problems being as serious as they are and the only solution society is willing to pursue being "lock 'em up," there is an incredible backlog in our courts.

Flaco is ordinarily nervous, but when he entered court after waiting in jail for a whole year, he appeared even more uptight. And who could blame him? His whole life was on the line. The charge was murder, and if he was convicted he faced at least twenty years, probably more.

I sat near him and his lawyer in the courtroom and could sense the strain Flaco was under. This was a bench trial before a judge alone without a jury. Not twelve people to decide your fate—just one—and Flaco undoubtedly would have to take the stand and tell his whereabouts at the time of a street drive-by shooting on Chicago's Near North side.

The year in jail had been hard on Flaco, but some good things had happened, too. Friends brought him to our weekly youth service and counseling sessions, and he had come to know the Lord, an experience that filled the void in his life he had tried so hard to satisfy with partying and peer acceptance from the gang. For that he was grateful and knew the changes Christ had made in his life. Still, he had read enough of the Bible to know that God did not usually pluck people out of their problems, even those who were innocent, and he had long since quit telling God how the verdict had to come out. He was braced to accept whatever it was, win or lose.

Yet he never wavered in insisting on his innocence. The state had to prove him guilty, and they had little to go on. No weapon, only a photo identification of Flaco from an eyewitness. But that witness had written on the back of the picture, "I'm not sure." In court, the witness said the same thing: the gunman he had seen looked like Flaco, but he was not sure. Furthermore, the arresting police officer could not remember taking a statement from Flaco until it was shown to him. But when it was read into the record, it contained no reference to the crime at all. It was merely an alibi defense of where Flaco had been at the time of the shooting. Then the state rested.

The judge threw the case out of court without even calling on Flaco and his lawyer to present a defense. Flaco was elated and his friends in court erupted in cheers and applause. But a young man had just had a *year* of his life wasted in jail because of sloppy police work, a stubborn prosecutor, and a jammed court system that could not set the record straight sooner.

To his credit, Flaco did not let the incident make him bitter. Instead he thanked his attorney for his efforts and praised God for the victory.

SOMETIMES YOU CAN'T ESCAPE

After a year in jail, Flaco had finally experienced justice from the court. Others are not so fortunate. Our judicial system chooses not to consider what a man is today and how he may have changed but looks only at the offense he committed sometime in the past to decide how long he must serve. And it is at that point that we see new tragedies committed in our courts and correctional institutions.

Disby's mother, for instance, did not have it easy. She was raising a son and daughter alone, working hard to make ends meet, and trying—often futilely—to counteract the depressing environment on the North Side of Chicago where the family lived. Well-developed and unusually intelligent for a fourteen-year-old, Disby was eagerly recruited by a neighborhood gang and soon earned the name "Slick" for his daring ability to get out of tough street encounters. But he was also quite a ladies' man, nicely dressed with good manners and charm that won him admiring young girls, who found him much more considerate and sociable than the average street gang member. He was a boy a girl could take home to meet mother and know she would be favorably impressed, especially if Mom did not know that the colors on his sweater were gang colors.

One day after school, Disby was walking home with his girlfriend and one of her friends when—still in the school yard—they were confronted by three young rivals.

"Hey, girl," said Slim, the spokesman for the trio, to Disby's girlfriend, "take off that sweater. Those are our colors you're wearing."

She refused, and Disby told the boys to leave. "These girls have nothin' to do with gangs; they're just on their way home."

A shouting match erupted, followed by shoving. "We've got a piece,[2] and we'll shoot!" threatened Slim.

Disby had no reason to doubt the young men were armed. In many urban areas "bullies," "deathtraps," and "hole diggers"—commonly known as guns—are often as much the rage as faddish haircuts, team jackets, and Air Jordans®.[3]

Immediately concerned for his safety and that of the girls, Disby pulled out a gun and fired. Slim was killed and another rival wounded. Disby was charged with murder and attempted

2. A gun.
3. Gordon Witkin, "Kids Who Kill," *U.S. News and World Report*, 8 April 1991, p. 31.

murder. Ironically the rivals had been bluffing; they had no weapon.

At the detention center Disby came to the chapel programs and Bible studies. Soon his curiosity about the Lord turned into a commitment of faith that began the process of turning his life around. He had a long wait in custody and lots of time to read and study, which he did eagerly.

The juvenile court judge decided Disby would be tried as an adult, a rather unusual decision for a teenager with little history of legal trouble. But at least he was finally released on bail after his family gathered together the needed funds.

While he was in custody, his mother had moved to a suburban community and rented a nice apartment. Out on bail, Disby began attending an outstanding high school—Oak Park/River Forest—and became active in YFC's Campus Life ministry; he also often attended church with me. It was quite a turnabout. The life on the streets was behind him. He was a typical high school student, doing well in some classes and not in others. The problems he and his mother dealt with were typical: curfew, homework, clothing styles, and helping out around the house. The gang wars on the streets seemed long gone. Faculty, students, and their parents who met Disby at his new school would have been amazed to learn that this friendly youth was actually awaiting trial on a murder charge.

Eventually the trial came, and Disby and the girls both testified that the victims *said* they had a gun and would use it. Disby believed their lives were in danger, so he had shot before he and his friends could be hurt or killed. The state, however, said it had been a deliberate killing by a youth anxious to show off in front of the girls. The issue was clear: self-defense, with Disby's only crime the carrying of a gun (not excusable but not uncommon), or a deliberate, cold-blooded homicide.

It was a hard choice for the jury, and they finally decided on middle ground: second-degree murder, a manslaughter conviction. The range of sentences on that charge is wide, all the way from probation to fifteen years in prison.

Disby's capable public defender prepared carefully for the sentencing hearing, pointing out the questionable circumstances of the shooting and the decision the jury had reached. He also told the judge of Disby's progress, all the efforts his mother had made successfully in the year the case was pending trial, testimony I supported on the witness stand. Finally Disby himself stated that he was very sorry about what happened that fateful day, and he was now far from that old lifestyle and neighborhood. The prosecutor had little to say, other than to indicate that a youth had died in the incident and Disby had had a run-in with one of the coaches at his new high school that resulted in a disciplinary suspension. Perhaps the state's attorney believed he did not have to present much of an argument at the sentencing—that the judge was already on his side. He was right.

The hostility the judge had managed to hide all through the trial burst out as he angrily attacked the jury's decision as "irresponsible."

"You fooled that jury, but you aren't fooling me," he said. "This was a first-degree murder case all the way. Probation? A short sentence? Forget it! I regret the law says I can only give you fifteen years in prison, but that is what the sentence will be."

Disby is now serving that sentence.

He will be eligible for parole in seven-and-a-half years if an appeal court does not intervene. He will come out with training and a license to work in the plumbing trade. But all the gang influences his mother worked so hard to get him away from surround him in prison; all the old pressures are there.

Hopefully, with his faith in the Lord, Disby will survive the experience and not come out of prison worse than when he went in, as happens to too many young convicts. Only time will tell.

THE HIGH COST OF PRISON

Prosecutors and judges see how gang and drug addictions destroy kids, but not knowing how to reverse the trend they mandate longer and longer confinement. Legislators and courts attempt to manufacture consequences as a deterrent but do their work so inequitably as to make the results meaningless yet costly. The system becomes irrelevant and destructive rather than accomplishing society's goals and hopes. The alarming rates of recidivism in our courts and institutions shout the failure of the get-tough and throw-the-key-away philosophies.

Trying younger kids in adult courts, throwing them in prison, and locking them up longer is popular today. But most often it wastes lives and dollars in costly failure. The Illinois Juvenile Justice Commission reports that as of 1991 it cost $34,053 to confine a youth in a state correctional facility (about the nationwide average). In some states it costs more. The Hickey Training School for Boys on the edge of Baltimore, an end-of-the-line lock-up for 350 hardened youths, costs $60,000 for each ward. At Hickey there is one hour of recreation on weekdays and none on weekends. Interscholastic sports are ancient history, and all pretense of rehabilitation and treatment has been dropped as the school confronts an epidemic of escapes as well as personnel and fiscal fiascoes.

Consider Ferris, the Delaware State Reformatory, which spends $65,000 a year on each inmate (85 percent of it on staff salaries), where there has been a steady string of rioting and attempted suicide. That is fairly typical of facilities across the nation. And yet prosecutors insist that kids be put in institutions, and judges acquiesce with sentences to such places that are destructive to their young charges and that these court officers have never visited.

On a more positive note is the program at Glen Mills School near Philadelphia, which houses 800 young residents with histories of violence, manipulation, and drug dealing. At Glen Mills they believe delinquency is the norm in the milieu from which these kids come, and they are right. Inner-city kids gain their recognition on the streets, not the school campus. The Glen Mills staff affirms the normal needs of kids for identity and accomplishment but seeks to change the *means* by making educational, vocational, and athletic achievement the path to recognition. They have seen some dramatic success. Their efforts contrast starkly with the normal treatment mode based on delinquency as an emotional disorder.

The youth correctional programs in Illinois fall somewhere between the extremes. But they still do not follow the law, which states in effect, "Juvenile offenders shall be placed in a rehabilitation program designed to return them to the community as good citizens with the least confinement and shortest possible time away from home." Instead, when the judge "commits" the young offender to the department of corrections, the state parole board confines him (or her) for a set time based on the offense committed, whether or not that is the most rehabilitative option.

Illinois also mandates that for certain of the most serious crimes, juveniles fifteen years old and up *must* be tried as adults; in addition the judge has the *option* of trying them as adults at age thirteen. Illinois, alone among the states with a mandatory transfer to adult court for youths on serious charges, permits no review of that transfer by either the juvenile or criminal courts. The policy is politically popular but tremendously destructive to young people. As one juvenile court official told me, "By such transfers we sacrifice several hundred kids a year on the altar of political expediency."

Why? In looking for solutions, are we relying on a "corrections" system that punishes at best, commonly exacerbates the problem by throwing youth in prison where they must cooperate with gang rule to survive, and is a miscarriage of justice at worst?

It is increasingly apparent that only as a community brings *all* its resources together can the problem be confronted with any hope of making a difference: police, probation, courts, schools, recreation, jobs and job training, counseling, correctional institutions, and churches all need to be on the team together, not each going its own way. Everyone in the field believes that this *should* happen, but it is not. Why are the people and institutions who should be part of the solution often part of the problem instead?

9

Youth at Risk

Nationally the pattern of arrests per capita among youthful offenders has actually remained steady in the last ten years, according to the National Council on Crime and Delinquency.[1] However, the *seriousness* of offenses has increased. A generation ago the juvenile court confronted the truant, the petty thief, and the joyrider who stole a car. Today's young offender may carry a Tec-9, Raven P-25, AK-47, or Uzi and not hesitate to use it. He will be charged with homicide, attempted murder, rape, or drug sales.

Discussing the seriousness of youthful arrests a veteran police officer said, "The thing that scares me most is these kids can commit the most violent acts and then stop and eat or listen to music with their friends as if nothing happened. They seem totally devoid of feeling or care for anyone else." This certainly seemed to be the case with Demetrius.

CAUSE TO CELEBRATE?

Eighteen-year-old Demetrius was considered the prime instigator when five young men picked up a girl at a party, gang-raped her, brutally stabbed her again and again, and then

1. Stated in a report by the National Council on Crime and Delinquency (NCCD) for the Illinois Department of Corrrections in September 1990.

ran over her broken body with their car. It was a heinous and revolting crime.

When he was arrested, Demetrius simply transferred his power role on the streets to the jail deck, power he quickly attained. Nobody had anything good to say about Demetrius. He was surly, foul-mouthed, and cold; the charges against him only added to that revulsion.

Even though he started coming to our services, I did not expect Demetrius to change, and frankly, considering the crime he had committed, neither did I care. But this young man began to do the unthinkable: he learned to read and began reading the Bible—a book I was sure he viewed with indifference, if not outright rejection of all it said about morality and the sacredness of life.

His cousin Curt kept assuring me Demetrius was changing. "Sure," I replied, "and the head of the Mafia is being nominated for sainthood." Curt was one thing—a gentle, polite scholar heading for a career in the Air Force, who to everyone's surprise was also charged in this case—but Demetrius was another. I saw no redemptive potential in him.

Demetrius knew how I felt about him. He did not try to convince me, he just continued coming to our meetings, reading the Bible, and letting his influence on the jail deck be felt. For a long time I did not see the changes because I did not want to. If God wanted to forgive the likes of this cold rapist-killer, He could, but I would just as soon not be involved. But soon not only I but even the jail staff had to admit the obvious: Demetrius *was* changing.

It was amazing to watch a youth whose conscience had been so dormant that he was labeled sociopathic—incapable of genuine feelings or learning from experience—slowly start to come alive. As his body and mind began getting rid of the effects of alcohol and drugs, he began to think and reason and start to care for others, seeking not just his own pleasure or what they could do for him but seeking the good of others.

From a loner uninvolved in the activities or crosscurrents of emotion so prevalent in a place of close confinement, Demetrius became a player, then an active participant, and finally a leader in the group. Though everyone expected his influence to be negative, this young man helped, calmed, and encouraged others on his jail deck. He was well into this new direction before I even realized it was happening, I had so little contact with or concern for him.

When he and I finally did start talking, he wanted to know all I could teach him from the Bible. He was not given to making speeches or pointing to himself; he just quietly kept growing as a man and as a believer. As we met together, a childhood history of abuse and neglect in the home gradually unfolded. I glimpsed the incredible lure of alcohol and drugs to deaden the years of pain and give a false sense of well-being and the terrible effects chemical abuse had had on him—none of which excused his conduct but did help me begin to understand the influences that so totally warped and destroyed him.

At their trial both Curt and Demetrius were found guilty of murder and sexual assault. Curt was sentenced to natural life in prison without parole. Demetrius was sentenced to die.

Demetrius worked hard preparing what he would say to the judge at his sentencing. He wanted to express his sorrow for the tragedy and remorse he felt for the wrong he had done; he planned to state that he had asked the Lord's forgiveness and wanted to help, instead of hurt, people. He never got a chance. Every defendant in Illinois can make a statement to the judge before sentence is pronounced—except one facing a death sentence. The prosecution objected to Demetrius's being heard, and he was not.

The courtroom emptied quickly after the sentences were pronounced. Demetrius's lawyer and I were suddenly alone. He struggled for words. "This is my first major case in private practice," he said finally. "I was a prosecutor until recently, in charge of the unit trying death penalty cases. The two D.A.s who got the verdict today were my men; I taught them most of what they used so effectively. Before I left that office, we tried ten death penalty cases and got seven death verdicts. Each time I was elated, and each time we celebrated."

He paused a few moments, then continued. "Now I'm on the other side. It's not just that I lost; in law you win and you lose. But this is a young man's life, and I know him. The jury decided he did a terrible wrong and must die—but he's not a 'depraved animal' as the state's attorneys called him. Demetrius is capable of improving himself and becoming a better person. And he can do some good for others, even serving time in prison. But he helps neither himself nor anyone else when he's buried."

The lawyer put his papers in his brief case and wearily got up from the defense counsel's table. "Maybe the same is true of the seven men in whose cases I got death penalties. The lawyers I formerly worked with are out celebrating now; a few months back I would have been with them, accepting the enthusiastic congratulations of our colleagues. Today it makes me sick."

He didn't wait for a response but quickly turned and left the courtroom.

On Demetrius's arrival on death row at Menard Prison, he was one of the two youngest inmates in the state awaiting the maximum penalty. As I pray for him, his family, and the family of his victim, I only wish the chance to confront Demetrius with the good news of the gospel had come long before he sat in a jail chapel service. Just possibly things might have turned out differently.

BEHIND THE HEADLINES

The wrong things a youth does make headlines. The reader shudders and is glad that these violent youths are "put away." But behind the headlines are young people at risk, for whom it is just a matter of time until many are themselves victims of drug or alcohol abuse or violence, or are incarcerated.

The risks of growing up in America today are compounding. It does not take a lot of statistics to see that the American family is in serious trouble. Andrew Edwards of Cleveland State University writes, "The use of illicit drugs, teenage rebellious activity, domestic violence, irresponsible sexual behavior, individual depression, chronic anxiety, and certain other emotional disturbances are often termed *social pathology* (or sickness or deviance). However, it is erroneous to view the above as 'social problems.' All of the above are *symptoms* of a problem. The problem is FAMILY DYSFUNCTION."[2]

2. Andrew Edwards, "The Black Family: A Unique Social System in Transition," in *The State of Black Cleveland 1989* (Cleveland: Urban League of Greater Cleveland, June 1989), p. 192.

Others, of course, see the family as the victim of unprece-dented stress. Racial discrimination, poverty and unemploy-ment, inferior education, hopelessness, the abuse of illegal drugs, permissive attitudes toward sexual activity—all togeth-er put severe pressure on the family.

One significant problem impacting the family is the rise in the number of single parents trying to do the herculean task of raising and supporting kids alone. Both the growing number of children born to unmarried girls or women and the high di-vorce rate mean that roughly 50 percent of all kids spend at least part of their growing up years without one of their par-ents—usually their father.

Urie Bronfenbrenner, a child development expert at Cor-nell University, has linked "father absence" to a number of se-rious problems common among youths in the inner city, such as "low motivation for achievement, inability to defer immedi-ate rewards for later benefits, low self-esteem, susceptibility to group influence . . . and juvenile delinquency."[3]

Whichever comes first—the "chicken" or the "egg," mod-ern social pressures or family dysfunction—what's happening in the home is a key factor in what's happening with our youth on the streets. Parents often do not know what to do with a growing adolescent on troubled streets—and some frankly don't care. And all too often the parents *do* know what the kid is doing.

One young dope dealer told me he gave his mother a com-plete dining-room and living-room set for Christmas that cost $6,000. Did his mother ask where the money came from? "No," he honestly replied. "She just hugged me and thanked me for such a nice present." What is going through some parents' minds? When a kid comes home with new $125 gym shoes or an equally expensive jacket or gold chains or a motorcycle, it should occur to parents to ask where the money came from.

Charles, a nice looking boy with a big smile, was in juve-nile detention again, this time caught with another boy in the act of burglarizing a school. His mother and older brother

3. *Family Policy*, September/October 1989, a publication of the Family Re-search Council, quoting Andrew Oldenquist, *The Non-Suicidal Society* (Bloomington, Ind.: Indiana U., 1986).

came to juvenile court to tell the judge how concerned they both were about Charles's behavior. After court I told Charles how fortunate he was to have two people who cared that much for him.

He laughed. "Do you want me to tell you what *really* happened, Rev?" he asked. "Everything I steal I bring home to my mother, and she gets pretty angry if I haven't made a good haul at a shopping center. As for my older brother, he is on parole from prison, so he can't afford to get caught. He was acting as lookout at the school when the police showed up, so he made up this story about going down there to find me because he heard I was going to the school late at night. They believed him, too—that's the amazing thing. *Now* what would you like to say about my family?"

I admitted I had been fooled but said, "Then you need to be a better person than they are, Charles, and you have all the ability and chance to do so." It took several years and a number of trips in and out of detention for him to realize he could choose a new way, but he eventually did. Charles has moved away, lives in another city, has a wife and little daughter of his own, works for his money, and is doing well. But no thanks are due to his mother and brother.

Unfortunately some little kids, seven or eight years old, are "pee-wees" in the same gangs their fathers or older brothers belong to. That's a cycle that's hard—though not impossible—to break. Almost worse are the parents who put on a nice front of respectability and concern, yet behind the facade are destroying their children by attitudes of cold rejection and impossible standards. These parents are described well in the book on family evil, *People of the Lie*, by psychologist Scott Peck.[4]

NOT JUST ANOTHER STATISTIC

Behind all the statistics are real stories and hurting people. Rachel's parents said she ran away from home; she said she was forced out. That was not the only thing they disagreed on, but in this instance both of them may have been right.

4. M. Scott Peck, *People of the Lie* (New York: Simon and Schuster, 1983).

I met Rachel at the juvenile detention center in Chicago, and even the drab institutional clothing could not hide her natural attractiveness. But it was soon apparent that her smile was merely surface covering for a well of deep hurt underneath. She had reached out for love to the two most important people in her life, her mother and father, and was greeted with a cruelty hard for her to describe.

Rachel's parents both had problems with alcohol. Her mother took pills to try coping with that problem only to create another. A sympathetic grade-school teacher alerted the authorities that Rachel was coming to school tired, depressed, and not having eaten properly. Children's services took her out of the home, placed her in foster care, and worked at getting the parents into counseling.

There are good and bad foster homes; though the one chosen for Rachel was a distinct improvement over her own home, it still left much to be desired. Put simply, the foster parents wanted state money—they spent as little as they could on Rachel and offered her even less in terms of emotional support. She soon ran away and ended up on Chicago streets. Her welcoming committee was a few gang youths looking for some partying companions with whom they could share their marijuana and beer. She was considered an excellent pickup.

Rachel mistook their attention for affection and ended up in bed with one of the boys after a night of partying. The next day a police officer stopped the group, learned she did not live in the area and, when she did not mention the foster home, returned her to her parents.

They seemed glad to have her come back, especially since Rachel indicated that she wanted to try again at home. They felt it might get the caseworkers off their back. However, all the parents' promises of change and a fresh start evaporated during the next alcohol binge, and the pattern of verbal abuse and physical assaults began anew. Eventually Rachel left home, this time to be picked up for shoplifting at a department store.

She was held at the detention center pending disposition of her case, attending the center school as well as the voluntary Bible classes and chapel services. She knew little about God; mostly she had heard His name used by her parents as a swear word. That God was concerned about her and wanted to re-make her into a successful, happy person was beyond the realm of her imagination.

Still she did read the Bible the chapel volunteers gave her and looked forward to the discussion groups and services. She began to understand that God's Father-love was not the "love" her parents had shown—erratic, inadequate, cruel—but rather a compassion that offered her security and strength. Perhaps the most wonderful offer she had ever heard was the Lord's words "Come to me, all you who are weary and burdened, and I will give you rest" (Matthew 11:28). When Rachel decided to trust Him, she received much more than a momentary consolation or even a sympathetic shoulder on which to cry. She was born into God's family in a new relationship with Him that offered more hope than she had ever known in her fifteen years of life.

But there was something she wanted God to do more than anything else: that her parents would also find the Lord. She kept asking the chapel teams to pray that her family could be reunited. Those wishes do not always lead to a happy ending; everyone must make his or her own choice, and no matter how much a child wants her parents to change—or the other way around—sometimes it just does not happen. So while they prayed with Rachel, the chapel staff was careful to build her trust in the Lord rather than in a magical turnaround with her parents.

At court Rachel asked to go home for one more try, and a reluctant judge agreed, providing there was close supervision and counseling of the family. Rachel invited her parents to go to church with her, an experience neither parent had had since childhood. But because they saw how earnest she was and the strength her faith had given her, they agreed. An alert, kindly pastor followed up by calling on the family, and eventually they all united with the church following their public commitment to the Lord.

Besides getting involved in her church youth program, Rachel also got some excellent support from *Alanon*, a program for family members of alcoholics. Meanwhile her parents began attending group sessions of *Parents Anonymous*,[5] which helps mothers and fathers who want to stop abusing their children as well as those who want to get help before they start.

DRUGS: THE NEW PLAGUE

Unfortunately, Rachel's story is the exception, not the rule. In the war on drugs, drugs are winning, especially in the inner city.

Cocaine comes from all over the world, frustrating our much vaunted war on drugs, in which the forces of law and order are outnumbered, outspent, and outgunned many times over by the international syndicates. Because a major part of the economies of Colombia, Peru, Bolivia, and increasingly Brazil are based on drug sales, totally eradicating the cocaine trade from those countries would bankrupt them. The international bankers to whom those countries owe debts in the billions are not likely to allow that to happen.

In the U.S. the dope dealers insist that they are just meeting a market demand. All they are doing is finding customers and supplying them. But *Ebony* magazine hit the mark when it wrote that an entire generation is at risk because of the "drug cancer," not only through addiction and health-related issues such as AIDS, "but illegal drug use is either directly or indirectly related to much of the crime that plagues the black community."[6]

In many of our inner cities, the terms "gang member" and "drug dealer" are almost synonymous. Gangs compete for the drug market, increasing deadly violence between rivals, with many innocent young people caught in the crossfire. Even worse, drug trafficking has moved into the schools. Though gang members in general are not easy to identify, unless they choose to parade their gang colors or other distinctive dress, drug dealers often flaunt their wealth. "For young kids grow-

5. In the U.S., except California, phone 800/421-0353; in California, phone 800/352-0386.
6. "Massive Abuse of Illegal Drugs Must Be Stopped," *Ebony*, August 1986, p. 149.

ing up in poverty, seeing the older kids with sudden wealth becomes a stimulus for them to become involved in drugs."[7]

In desperation, some have argued for legalizing illicit drugs, a short-sighted response that would bring far more serious problems than it would ever solve. Those who advocate legalization forget that a high percentage of the users are *not* adults. Are they prepared to make these dangerous drugs legally available to our children? Of course not, so we would still be left with a major, illegal drug trade. Treating legal addicts would cost an enormous amount, and because drug addicts are great spreaders of their plague, the number needing treatment would increase—a never-ending spiral of misery. And if we think drunk drivers and users of illegal drugs are a menace on the highway now, wait until drugs are legally available. Our highway death toll would be an even greater disaster than it is now. Legalizing drugs is *not* the answer; a united community response to the plague is.

Drug education helps; but drug education is most helpful when there are other life alternatives for youth: parental support, educational and job opportunities, attainable goals—options more likely to exist in the suburbs or among the middle class. As drug use drops in the suburbs, however, general interest in the problem will wane, leaving the youth most at risk in the inner cities to a certain fate.

POVERTY AND UNEMPLOYMENT

Even those youth who would like to get a job face overwhelming barriers, especially in the inner city. Many of the available jobs are out in the suburbs, so transportation itself is a major hurdle. And in spite of civil-rights legislation, unemployment rates for minorities have been consistently double those for whites—and they are rising. For instance, in 1985 the jobless rate for blacks was 15.1 percent but only 6.2 percent for whites.[8]

We cannot ignore that economics plays a significant role in the stability of the family. Statistics for one minority group

7. Ibid.
8. "Special issue: The Crisis of the Black Family," *Ebony*, August 1986, p. 37.

in 1983 show that only 29 percent of poor black families had both a father and a mother in the home, whereas 80 percent of nonpoor black families were two-parent families.[9] The Family Research Council recently reported that "a significant decline in the earning power of young black men has contributed significantly to the retreat from marriage and the rise of illegitimacy during the last fifteen years."[10]

When a minority teenager surveys the job scene—or lack of it—and the formidable barriers to be overcome (finishing high school, money for college, the unemployment rate, poor job training and skills), is it any wonder the temptation to make big bucks by dealing drugs is luring more and more kids? What chance does $4.50 an hour at MacDonalds have against fifty bucks just for being a lookout or $300 in an afternoon of dealing? It takes strong family and personal values to resist the temptation and set long-term goals, values that have been seriously weakened in the social and family structure of our inner cities.

In my experience with kids on the streets and in our correctional institutions, three words characterize the nineties for these youth: anger, fear, and despair. Many, if not most, of them feel, "I'll never make it—so why not live for today?"

Why not indeed? We—you and I—have an answer. Because Christ died for these kids, He cares about every single one of them—those on the streets, those in the jails. God cares about the lives that are being wasted, the pain and violence wreaking havoc in families. Through Christ these lives can be redeemed to be productive citizens and role models, helping other kids choose a different path. But it is not going to happen unless we admit that what is happening on the streets of our cities and in our suburban neighborhoods is our problem, too.

WHERE IS THE CHURCH?

Mike took me for a ride through several suburban communities near Chicago to show me streets he knew well. A few

---

9. Statistics from "Understanding African-American Family Diversity," in *The State of Black America 1990* (National Urban League, 1990), pp. 97-99.
10. "Restoring the Black Family," Family Policy, a publication of the Family Research Council, September/October 1989.

years back he had started branches of his street gang in these same areas. He had found recruiting easy, and we now saw well-established gang graffiti on walls in pleasant communities with nice homes, occupied by many people who had left the city to escape just such problems.

Ironically Mike's family was among them. Both of his parents worked hard to save money so they could move to a nice area miles away from trouble. But with Mike and his three brothers active in gangs, the trouble came with them, and eventually the family returned to the city. There three of the four boys were shot in separate shooting incidents. In concern for the boys' safety, the parents moved out to the suburbs again. By this time Mike was sobered by what had happened to his brothers and wanted to cool his gang participation. But in trying to keep one of his brothers out of trouble, Mike was shot on the steps of their new home and remained unconscious for thirty-four days before making a long, slow recovery.

Realizing that he had been given another chance and with a newfound faith giving him a new direction, Mike does not plan to return to the wars of the streets. But he is concerned for the young kids he readily brought into the gang.

Even though their parents could afford to move to nicer communities, being accepted socially in the schools and by the other teens was another matter. "These kids were looking for the identity they'd lost in moving from the city," Mike explained. "They just wanted action, power, and quick money, and we provided it." Gang affiliation gave these minority youth a way of holding their own and even striking back at the entrenched Caucasian young people who did not accept the newcomers. Mike did not have to pressure new recruits to join; he had to screen the many eager applicants, a fact parents and community leaders find difficult to accept.

While we drove through one area intense with gang activity, I noticed an evangelical church at the end of the block. A few days later I called on the youth minister at that church. He told me the church congregation consisted primarily of whites who no longer lived in the area but had moved still farther out to yet better suburbs. "The church has little contact or involvement with the kids living around here," he admitted.

I nodded. "I'd like to take you to the heart of local gang territory."

Curious, he agreed. "Shall we drive in my car?" he asked.

"There's no need," I said. "We can easily walk; it's only in the next block." As we walked that street well within sight of his church, we were in a different world than he realized existed and for which his church had no outreach and, frankly, little concern. But perhaps out of our tour, the seeds of vision for reaching kids in their own neighborhood may start.

Part 4

WHAT NEEDS TO HAPPEN

10

Change in the System

Some police departments are trying innovative approaches to dealing with the problems of the young. The CRASH unit in Los Angeles (Community Resources Against Street Hoodlums) is one such effort targeting key gang areas for special enforcement. In communities as diverse as New York, Chicago, Baltimore, and Newport, police are getting out of their cars and patrolling the streets on foot. In Seattle, Tulsa, Toronto, and Lombard, Illinois, they are successfully using bicycles to collar young gangbangers and thieves.

As I speak at seminars with the International Juvenile Officers Association, I am finding communities increasingly combining their police resources and working together to combat a menace that never stops at a city border. These officials are finding that answers do not come easy: schools are often inadequate, the criminal justice system frequently breaks down on sheer volume alone, jobs for kids where they are most needed are nonexistent, and recreational areas become gang battlefields. Police are also caught between a community demanding that the hoodlums cleaned out and the legal restraints of civil rights designed to prevent abuse of police power.

But as a concerned citizen—as a concerned Christian—what can you do? In this chapter I want to talk about attitudes that lead to helpful changes in the system. Too few people in our society are informed about the facts and the options. Therefore, they are quickly motivated in directions that, though popular, do not produce satisfactory long-term solutions.

THE COST OF INCARCERATION

Locking up people is not the only solution. In the last fifteen years the State of Illinois spent $536 million to build fifteen new medium- and minimum-security prisons. Unfortunately, during that same period, the state's prison population (among the fastest growing in the nation) almost tripled and now totals more than 28,000 prisoners, partially as a result of an increasing "get-tough" policy.[1]

Illinois's Pontiac Correctional Center is an example of the product of this policy. Dan Jarrett, president of the guard union says, "Right now, the inmate gangs . . . have more control over the institution than the staff." Consequently in 1990 there were reported 257 inmate attacks on inmates and 331 inmate attacks on staff.[2]

To regain control from the gangs, at least thirty-six other states have chosen to build some form of supermaximum-security prisons at an average of more than $100,000 per cell.[3] The theory is to isolate the most predatory inmates from the general prison population, often confining them to their cells twenty-three hours a day. California—where the inmate population is as violent and gang-troubled as in Illinois—built supermaximum units as part of a ten-year, $4.4 billion prison building program. Its supermaximum Pelican Bay prison unit was completed in 1989. "We decided that we just couldn't let the gangs run the place anymore, so they decided to take back control," said Carl Larson, who oversees prison design in California. Inmates are assigned there only for causing problems inside other prisons. Gang leaders are a priority. Larson says, "Some

1. Rob Karwath, "Taxpayers Foot the Bill for Packed Prisons," *Chicago Tribune*, 2 April 1991, pp. 1, 14.
2. Wes Smith, "State's Prisons Test the Limits," *Chicago Tribune*, 31 March 1991, pp. 1, 13.
3. Wes Smith, "State Puts Low Priority on High-Security Prison," *Chicago Tribune*, 1 April 1991, p. 1.

wardens say that their work has become a piece of cake because when inmates act up, all they have to do is mention Pelican Bay."[4]

And how has the country's propensity for quick incarceration deterred the growth of gangs? A 1990 University of Chicago study of forty-five cities reported 1,439 gangs with 120,636 members. A nationwide survey for *Parade Magazine* found the problem growing in many locations. Boston, with six known gangs in 1987, now has twenty-five. Between 1984 and 1988, Miami's four gangs grew to sixty, with more than 3,000 members. Seattle is trying to cope with fifty mostly new gangs. Milwaukee reports 4,000 gang members, Denver 3,000, Phoenix 2,000. Los Angeles reports membership up 100 percent since 1985. Tragically the average age of gang members—which was fifteen in 1984—has dropped to thirteen and a half today.[5]

Many people believe that the goal of rehabilitating offenders is naive, that it just does not work. So they have reverted to the view that our criminal justice system's first task is to punish criminals and thereby to hopefully deter potential offenders. But rehabilitation was never genuinely tried, and though the thought of prison may seem abhorrent to law-abiding citizens, it has not been shown to be an effective deterrent to those inclined toward crime. Please do not misunderstand me. I believe in holding offenders accountable for their conduct, but a narrow punishment mode may be inadequate.

BUT WHAT ABOUT PUNISHMENT?

The criminal justice system is built around a punishment mode: a certain offense calls for a certain time served, often with little or no consideration for the age, maturity, or motive of the offender. Even the juvenile court, which was founded with the goal of encouraging rehabilitation, has gotten onto the same punishment track. Court officials will frequently say, "I know this sentence won't deter anyone, I don't think it will

4. Ibid., p. 9.
5. Al Santoli, "What Can Be Done About Teen Gangs?" *Parade Magazine*, 24 March 1991, p. 17.

lead to your rehabilitation, and it may not even help the victim. But a certain act calls for so much time behind bars, and that is what you're going to serve. It's just punishment."

That is a costly, foolish response on the part of society, especially with young offenders. It may be that those old and hardened enough to commit serious offenses should be put away to protect society (they constitute about 15 percent of our current prison population), but don't put naive, foolish young kids in with them.

The goal of the system needs to be to encourage self-rehabilitation (no one rehabilitates anyone else), using intensive probation supervision in the community, restitution, community service, education, and job-training programs as much as possible. Warehousing young people in expensive misery is a waste in most cases.

A profession of faith in the Lord should not form the basis for different treatment or leniency. However, an evident change of life in terms of attitude, motivation, conduct, self-improvement, and care for others—often the *results* of Christian conversion—needs to be considered when a judge makes a determination about what should happen to an offender.

Recently an independent study commissioned by Prison Fellowship concluded that prisoners who receive Christian training have significantly lower rates of re-arrest after release than those who receive no such training. John Gartner, the clinical psychologist who headed the research team, called the results "phenomenal. . . . No one before had ever looked at the effect of religion on recidivism. . . . There haven't been any findings of effectiveness that were this strong." The study found that the religion-trained offenders had a recidivism rate 11 percent lower than the control group. Plus they stayed crime-free longer, and if they did break the law, it was a less severe offense compared to their past crimes. The control group, on the other hand, exhibited increased crime severity.[6]

Even more striking is the situation in the Humaita Prison in Brazil. Charles Colson reports that for the past eighteen years the entire prison has been run by Christian volunteers

6. Associated Press, "Study Finds Religion Does Affect Convicts" *Chicago Tribune*, 30 November 1990.

(now a part of Prison Fellowship) who provide humane treatment and Christian instruction. Of the five hundred offenders who have been released from that prison over those years, only 4 percent have been returned to prison. That is in dramatic contrast to the 75 percent recidivism rate for other Brazilian institutions (also the world average).[7]

Certainly my own ministry is witness to the way Jesus can genuinely change a person, and Renegade is one example.

MIXED-UP VALUES

Renegade is fourteen years old. I met him in the juvenile detention center during his long stay there. He was attracted to the excitement and action of the urban streets before he reached his teen years. He is bright, has a nice appearance, and is well-spoken. He talks of caring for his mother and family.

As with many like him, he showed little regard for other people or their welfare. In his world being accepted by the older boys, getting in on the action, making some fast money was all that mattered. His views of right and wrong were sadly deficient; his respect for others close to rock bottom.

Many experts would say that he had a low self-image, a standard diagnosis of most street kids, but it certainly was not true here. He had a strong self-image, as well as confidence, *but for the wrong things and for the wrong reasons*. In his mixed-up values system, wrong was right, power and personal gain counted for everything, and being considered "bad" was the ultimate accolade. He had attained that status, so by *his* warped measuring gauge he was as successful as a Wall Street tycoon, a prominent politician, a famous athlete, or a million-dollar rock star.

My job: invade that wall of self-sufficiency to show him a need to change and then a way to do it. It was not an easy assignment. But I had several things to help me: he was intelligent; his freedom had been suddenly and drastically curtailed when he was locked up, and that situation could continue for a long time; he was smart enough to see where his way of life had gotten him. And there were two other factors he would never

7. Charles Colson, "The Secret Prisoner of Humaita Prison," *Christianity Today*, 8 April 1991, p. 96.

have considered (nor would most experts on delinquent youth): the power of the Holy Spirit to change a life and answers to the prayers of many believing, caring Christians who honored my request to pray for these youths I counseled each week.

The courts take no account of what a teenager is like if that system chooses to transfer him to adult court for trial. Though Renegade was one year short of the mandatory transfer age, the juvenile court did decide that he should go to adult court.

Then came the long months awaiting final court action. The judge presiding over Renegade's case basically had the choice, if the youth pleaded guilty, of sending him to prison for twenty to forty years. He was charged with shooting a rival in the face and killing him.

It is never my contention that leniency or some break should be given a kid because he is in a Bible study program or has made a profession of faith. But neither should the courts base their decisions only on a tragic incident that happened one night. People can—and do—change. And that change— brought about by a Christian conversion or some other means— should be important to a disposition.

Renegade and I took a hard look at his life and how he had gotten where he was. Against his initial indifference toward hurting a rival, I raised the issue of his reaction to someone who was hurting his mother or someone in his family. I got an expected quick and firm response followed by the realization that hurting others is wrong. His sense of morality, long dormant since childhood church experiences, began to come to life and produce a sense of guilt and responsibility that needed an answer.

Gang involvement is more than joining a club; it becomes a lifestyle, even an addiction. The youth surrenders his mind and values to the group and ends up doing things in a pack that he would never do alone. It is a life that starts out with excitement and ends in danger. A gang member feels that he has to carry a gun and even use it. As one said: "Better to be judged by twelve [a jury] than carried by six [pallbearers]."

Most of these kids do not even want to think about how gang life will end: dead too soon or in jail too long. And when they are caught up in the lure and excitement of the gang mentality, getting an education does not seem important, nor does working to earn "dead presidents" (money). Television, with its tendency toward violence, only reinforces antisocial attitudes and behavior. Fortunately for Renegade and his peers, there was another route to go.

That route was available through the infinite love of a dying Savior, and Renegade met Him. As well as the forgiveness he sought, there was the added benefit of an aroused conscience through the reading of God's Word, the strength to face discouragement and temptations, and even a sense of hope for the future despite his bleak legal situation.

Renegade and I prayed as he received the Lord into his life. I looked up to see the widest, happiest smile I have ever encountered. And it was far more than a surface change, he was eager to grow and learn all he could about his new life.

Renegade expects to serve time—twenty-eight years—but also plans to serve the Lord, continuing with his education and growing in faith. But it will not be an easy road.

The judge and the prosecutor knew Renegade as the boy who shot a rival in the face on the streets. I knew about that tragedy, but I also knew other things that had transpired since that fateful night in the public housing project when a life was taken, and bringing that side out certainly would not make the judge's decision any easier.

But part of a judge's job is to *judge* the person before the bench. If the violent, crazy act of one night determines guilt, certainly the long-range change in a person should be observable and taken into consideration in setting the sentence. And our legal system should accommodate and encourage that kind of discernment, not thwart it.

SOME NECESSARY LEGAL REFORMS

When you hear people talking casually about the need to crack down on crime, when political candidates promise the same, or when judges are up for re-election, be discerning about *what* and *whom* you endorse. Not every get-tough measure will help. Be brave enough to speak up. Be informed enough to vote intelligently. Here are several reforms I think could improve the way many states treat youthful offenders:

1. Urge speedier trials. Young people being tried as adults are often held far too long pending trial. Many times kids aged fourteen or fifteen are held a year or even two in "temporary" juvenile detention centers. Such a large percentage of a young person's total life (to date) cannot help but have a major negative impact on his personality, values, and outlook. If charges are reduced or dropped, the individual has endured a potentially embittering injustice.

2. Honor youths' civil rights. When young people are arrested for wearing what police consider gang colors and then released, or beaten and released because they have not committed some other illegal or prosecutable crime, they have been seriously violated. This behavior on the part of the police seldom intimidates or deters criminal behavior, but it certainly breeds angry, antisocial street kids.

3. Require public defenders to be on hand at police stations just as are state's attorneys when a minor is brought in on a serious charge. This could protect kids' rights and reduce police abuse, as well as false or forced confessions.

4. Revise accountability laws. If your state has or is considering an "accountability law" (making everyone in the company of someone who commits a crime equally guilty), review it carefully before numerous young people are snared into something much worse than they deserve.

5. Oppose mandatory transfers to adult courts. All states have provision to try some juveniles committing serious offenses as adults. A few, Illinois among them, *require* juveniles be tried as adults for certain crimes, and Illinois alone will not allow the juvenile court or the adult court to consider whether that is a good or bad decision, with the option of reversing it.

6. Eliminate mandatory prison sentences. In an attempt to thwart courtroom "deals" that allow vicious criminals to get off with light sentences, legislatures in forty-six states have instituted a list of mandatory sentences for specific crimes. It has not stopped the legal maneuvering; it has just moved the plea-bargaining earlier. But judges are prohibited by these laws from rendering more creative alternative sentences or using judicial discretion when the convicted person exhibits potential for reform. Furthermore, the policy is overcrowding our prisons and putting young inmates in expensive misery, many of whom could better pay back their debt to society by working at jobs and serving in the community.

7. *Rescind the death penalty for minors.* Twenty-two of our states allow for the execution of those under the age of eighteen. Young offenders can commit some heinous crimes, but this is a very young age to conclude that they are so twisted as to be beyond redemption.

8. *Insure that young offenders can clear their record.* Once a young offender has successfully completed his or her time and parole the law should provide for the person's record to be sealed and expunged so that career, military, and other opportunities are not thwarted. Another route is to defer final sentencing until the defendant has served a sentence, completed counseling, served restitution, or performed community service and then have the original charge dismissed.

I am not suggesting that we "go soft" on the "really bad dude" who commits a heinous crime, shows no remorse, and does not care. In that instance I, too, say lock him up to protect us all. But do not decide that all kids charged with serious crimes are in that category; they are not. The system needs to call for much more discretion on the part of judges. Mandatory sentences ordered by legislatures, no parole, adult court for juveniles—all the "get tough" policies are self-defeating. There need to be alternatives.

Correctional Alternatives

All people, including the young offenders to whom I minister, must be held accountable and responsible for their conduct and actions. The courts should do that, and the Bible teaches it. Feeling sorry for those caught up in unfortunate circumstances will not solve their problems; offering sympathy without insisting on responsibility only perpetuates the problems in an immature person and delays his or her great need to face reality.

The question is not, Should these young people be held responsible for what they have done? but rather, Where and how should that accountability come? Insisting on high bail or no bail release pending trial for young defendants—as some community groups demand—denies the principle of innocent until proven guilty. The emphasis must be on restitution to victims, not just confinement. Throwing the stiffest sentences at offenders because it is politically palatable is self-defeating and often makes the problem worse. What are some of the alternatives?

PRISON VS. DEATH

Even for the death penalty there are alternatives. A recent Amnesty International study showed that 69.1 percent of Kentucky residents support the death penalty. But when the alternative of a life sentence without parole was offered, support for the death penalty dropped to 36 percent.[8]

CIVIL SUITS

Far more realistic than criminal penalties can be civil action, where the victim's family takes the perpetrator to court and seeks damages. Many times, of course, there is no insurance or anything else of value that could cover an award, so the state must step in with victim compensation. These programs are in place but often are not generous enough in their awards and are burdened with long delays and red tape.

ELECTRONIC MONITORING

Several states are experimenting with a high-tech form of house arrest in which a convicted individual is required to wear a radio anklet that is tuned to a device in the person's home telephone. A computer automatically and randomly calls the person's home and checks whether the person is on the premises (within radio range). If the person is not there when he or she should be or if any tampering with the device is detected, officials are immediately notified. Violations could land the person behind bars. The program can be set to allow the person to be away from home for school or work or for other approved periods.

It has the twofold advantage of restricting an offender's freedom, either as a form of punishment or to break a pattern

8. From Illinois Coalition Against the Death Penalty newsletter, April/May 1990.

of hanging out with the wrong crowd, and of not putting the person in prison, where worse social damage can easily occur. It does not, however, prevent all criminal activity. A drug trafficker, for instance, could continue operating out of his house. Also, there is some danger that the device's convenience could become a source of abuse—too easily denying people their freedom simply because the method seems "humane."

INTENSIVE PROBATION PROGRAMS

Though it requires more personnel than electronic monitoring, intensive probation programs can be effective with some offenders. On the other hand, when the direct cost of incarcerating an offender is considered (not to mention the potential cost of teaching him to be a worse criminal), probation is quite cost effective.

SHORT-TERM SHOCK DISCIPLINARY CAMP PROGRAMS

These programs, sometimes dubbed "prison boot camps," can help some young offenders, but they are not a cure-all. They remove the individuals from an urban-type environment and put them through a rigorous physical and mental training regimen similar to military boot camp. They instill discipline, which can lead to a new and positive self-esteem, and can help create a respect for authority. They work best with young kids lacking these qualities. But not all gang members are deficient in these areas, and certainly the more hardened ones are not so easily impressed.

SPECIAL YOUTH CORRECTIONAL FACILITIES

While far from perfect, these are a great deal better at dealing with young peoples' needs than the adult prison system.

VICTIM-OFFENDER RECONCILIATION PROGRAMS

The Mennonite church has pioneered reconciliation efforts through the Office of Criminal Justice for the Mennonite Central Committee based in Akron, Pennsylvania. One product has been some amazingly effective pilot Victim-Offender Reconciliation Programs. Ron Claassen, the VORP director in Fresno, California, explains that once a commitment to be constructive has been secured from each individual, three steps are needed: (1) recognizing the injustice—facts and feelings concerning the offense are shared and discussed; (2) restoring the equity—the offender is asked to make things right as much as possible, which may include returning property *plus* restitution through work/service to compensate for those aspects of the offense that cannot be set right; (3) making clear agreements for the future—it is often crucial for the victim to be assured that the offender does not intend to "do it again."

This kind of Christian ministry offers a compelling alternative to hate and revenge by reconciling offender and victim. The Scriptures say we should be agents of reconciliation (2 Corinthians 5:20), bringing people not only to the Lord but to peace with each other.

COMMUNITY RESPONSES

In Omaha the Mad Dads program has mobilized men in gang-infested areas to patrol streets, counsel kids, alert neighbors, and call police as problems arise. In the North Austin area of Chicago concerned citizens of the overwhelmingly black neighborhood have banded together to march against drug dealers, seek court orders shutting down dope spots, and hold police accountable to keep the pressure on. Two priests in Chicago, George Clements and Michael Pfleger, caused amusement when they first began to protest the availability of drug paraphernalia at local stores. But they and their parishioners were serious, getting legislation passed at the state level to stop the supply, marching to close drug houses, and opposing advertising that exploited minority youth and were designed to sell them alcoholic beverages and cigarettes. The five-hundred member strong African-American Men for Justice group in Chicago is working locally and nationally to reclaim communities and young men from drugs and street gangs. Pastor Carl Hardrick and Steve Holter, a former gang leader, now have an important ministry to gangs in Hartford, Connecticut.

These programs begin to focus at the root of the problem. But even if there were fair court systems, effective alternatives to damaging sentences, and active community responses, some kids would still get in trouble. Some would be acting out the effects of their broken or dysfunctional homes, but some would come from good homes with good chances for success in life. They need something more than an improved environment. Take, for example, the story of Mario.

EVERYTHING WAS NOT ENOUGH

Mario's goal was a spot on the U.S. Olympic diving team, and as a promising Whitney Young High School athlete he was wooed with scholarships to a number of the nation's finest colleges. A good student, he came from a respected family and lived in a nice section of the city. Mario carried in his pocket a first-class ticket on the road to success.

He was a good-looking kid, neat and clean-cut, compact and wiry. He dressed sharply in ties and jackets and slacks. He made a good impression.

But there was another Mario, a hidden side. Perhaps all the pressures on him to succeed were more than he could handle, or maybe as the honors stacked up he wanted to show his Hispanic buddies that at heart he was still one with them in the social rejection they felt. Whatever the reason, he was an active member of the Latin Brothers street gang, a role his admiring teachers and coaches never knew about. Afternoons and evenings he practiced on the diving board and in the pool. Nights he took to the swarming shadows.

"I guess he thought he could do it," said a detective for whom arresting and convicting Mario became an eighteen-month obsession. "The Olympics and the gang. It was like he thought he could have it both ways."

"I never suspected," said the school's diving coach and assistant principal. "He was one of the best divers I've ever seen. He was beautiful, Olympic caliber. I never saw indications of any gang activity. I never even saw him lose his temper."

But to the cops he was known as a shooter, a trigger man, and a suspect in several assaults. On the street his name was mentioned with the respect born of fear.

In whatever he did he went all out, and as I commented to reporters probing Mario's history once he made headlines,

"The same drive that puts a man in *Who's Who* can put him on the most-wanted list."

After his eventual arrest and trial, witnesses testified that Mario lured his victim into a car pretending to be a member of a friendly gang. Then they said he drove the youth to an alley and killed him. It was a curbside execution, bloody and excessive, five shots point-blank from a sawed-off gun. He was found guilty. At his sentencing hearing his coaches testified to his ability, contribution to the team, and potential as a diver. It was not enough.

Late in the evening, in a deserted courthouse, the jury announced their decision: Mario was sentenced to death by lethal injection. As he awaits his appeal on death row at state prison, he still denies the charge and insists that he is innocent.

For the Marios of this world—as well as those who are more vulnerable to getting caught up in the violence of the streets—there is still something that can be done. While Mario was awaiting trial, he became one of the most active participants in our chapel and Bible study programs. He responded to the gospel message and took on a unique assignment in the jail school office: encouraging all new inmates coming in to get into the educational classes and helping arrange their study schedule. He did this eagerly, for rivals from the streets as well as for friends.

No matter what the outcome of his court appeal, hope has been introduced into Mario's life. And there is a way that you can be a part of that hope.

11

But What Can I Do?

The ten men and women from the pleasant suburbs west of Chicago were a little nervous. A few days earlier each had received an invitation in the mail to come to dinner in Little Village with some of the young leaders of the Two Six Nation; the letter was signed by two gang leaders. The prospective guests were told to park near a nice restaurant and "your cars will be safe . . . we think."

The guests enjoyed a fine, complimentary Mexican meal, and the boys talked informally with their guests as they ate. The visitors learned firsthand of the dangers, lures, and temptations for a kid growing up on urban streets, but they also found this group of young men quite different in another regard: all of them were in school or were working.

Louie, known on the streets as "the Player," introduced his boys and explained that he was going on to college and working in a travel bureau. Another of the boys, Sal, was in college, getting a degree in criminal justice and interning with the probation department.

"What happened that helped you beat the odds?" a curious businessman asked Louie.

Louie leaned back in his chair. "I was a sophomore in high school, caught up in life on the streets. One day some rivals stabbed me five times in the back at the entrance to Hubbard

High School. I spent some painful days in the hospital recovering. Gordon here"—he nodded to me—"had known me and my older brothers for several years and came to visit me at the hospital. We talked seriously about my future, something I hadn't thought about much before this. I also realized that it was the Lord who spared my life, and Gordon challenged me to consider my relationship with Him." That near-fatal experience became the turning point for Louis.

The suburban guests were impressed; this was a side of urban youth they rarely saw. But the evening was not over. After dinner I planned to take them a few blocks down the street for another unique experience: meeting with a group of young inmates in the Cook County Jail.

The boys at the restaurant were asked if they were going to accompany their guests to the jail. "No way!" replied Louie, "I don't want to get any closer to that place than I am now. Besides, it's in enemy territory."

A GLIMPSE INTO THE JAIL

The drive into the enclosure with its barbed-wire fences and the journey through a security check similar to that at an airport only with a metal detector that is much more sensitive, then through a maze of locked doors with identity checks at each, and finally into a multipurpose room that doubles as a gym and a chapel was in itself a sobering experience. This is not a tourist resort.

Seven young men were waiting for the visitors. They were much like the boys the group had met at dinner, only these kids were dressed in jail browns. They were housed in a special school wing in Division Six, along with 160 other teenage inmates awaiting trial. More than half faced murder charges and the rest a combination of heavy drug dealing and assault charges. Most were gang rivals from across the city and suburbs whose violent activities were brought to a sudden halt when they picked up a heavy case.[1] There is no middle ground here. These young men would either win their cases and go home, which happens for a fortunate few, or be convicted and sentenced to prison for terms as high as eighty years or even life.

1. Serious arrest charges.

"Many people believe you fellows go to the chapel services thinking you'll get out of your charges or get some break at court. Is that true?" asked one woman directly when the session was open for questions and comments.

"Let me answer that," volunteered Sam, a well-built young black man whose rugged features, marked by scars and tattoos, made him seem much older than his nineteen years. That he retained a positive outlook and a desire to contribute constructively to society was a credit to him and an even greater tribute to what the Lord was doing in his life. He is active in a weekly Bible study.

"I've already been to prison, got out, and picked up another case," he said. "Only this is one I didn't do. I've given my life to the Lord, and I want to serve Him, but I realize that has nothing to do with what happens in court. I'll be with the Lord no matter what the verdict; I spent too many years without Him to want to go back to that old way of life. God doesn't get us out of things or even make it easy on us because we know Him—I saw that when I read about three young Hebrew guys in the Bible who didn't do anything wrong but still ended up in a fiery furnace.[2] What He does do is go with us through anything that may come down, and that's what counts. As for my case, I expect to win it and get out. But either way I'm with Him."

Wydrick's situation was much different, and I did not know if he would tell our visitors what was ahead. He must have read my thoughts because he picked up where Sam finished.

"I go to court tomorrow to get my time, and I'm looking at a lot of years. Jesus isn't going to get me a time cut, but He will help my attitude and give me the strength to do what I have to do and be a better person. I came to know Him here; I only wish He and I had met on the bricks. A lot of things might be different now, and I wouldn't have made the big mistake that hurt someone else and messed up my life." (His sentence the next morning: fifty years.)

When the inmates were asked what happens at our Wednesday morning sessions, Martin spoke up. He is a feisty, aggressive street kid, still amazed at all the changes the Lord has made in his life. He's excited that our volunteers have estab-

2. Daniel 3:16-23.

lished a strong tie to his boys back on the street and that many of La Raza ("The Cause"), one of the fastest growing youth gangs in Chicago, have come to the Lord.

"When we come to chapel on Wednesdays, it's not just to get away from the cellblock or see our friends from other wings. Some guys may come for those reasons, and that's OK," Martin acknowledged. "What counts is not why they come but what they hear when they arrive. We have between forty and sixty guys, and Mr. McLean talks about what the Bible says and how it applies to our lives."

"They also come," I added, "because the volunteers and I make it clear we care for them. They need to know that we care about them before they care what we know. I tell a young inmate, 'I love you, not in some weird or perverted sense'—and these days it is necessary to use those exact words so as not to be misunderstood—'but I love you because God made you to be His, and He cares for you.' Often I can also add, 'I love the man you are becoming as God's Holy Spirit is working in your life since you trusted Him and started walking with Him.'"

"What is the response to the gospel message?" another visitor asked.

Jesus has already answered that question, so I referred to what He said in the fourth chapter of Mark's gospel. With some, Satan comes and snatches away the Word that was sown; others receive it with joy, but since they lack roots, they last only a short time, especially when there is trouble or persecution; with others the worries of this life and the deceitfulness of riches choke out the Word; and finally, some hear the Word, accept it, and produce a good spiritual harvest.

Those reactions are as typical today as they were in Jesus' days on earth. In fact, Scripture says that *all of us* "fall short of the glory of God" (Romans 3:23), which makes me uneasy at times, especially when I get to thinking how fortunate God is to have me on His team.

"We teach the Rev some things, too," Martin added. "We've got him onto the gangs in the Bible that he didn't know about. For instance, there were the Israel Boys and their leader, Sam, who were set up by the Philistine Guys and the head cheerleader of Philistine High School, Delilah." Smiles grew around the room. "In Jesus' time there were the Insane Bethlehem Maniacs, who were having a party at the Holiday Inn so there was no room for Joe and Mary to check in when she was expecting her child. Then there were the Herod Boys out to destroy the child and later another Herod, who tried Jesus on a rigged case; that Herod became the original Unknown Gutless Wonder. That king also put his boys around the cemetery to make sure Jesus didn't bust out; they were the Insane Grave Watchers. They didn't do much good, though, because Jesus busted out of the grave just like He said He would."

The seriousness in the room relaxed as the visitors enjoyed Martin's satire. But there was also a new light of understanding in their eyes.

"The important thing," commented Sam, "is we learn in a way we can understand that God can change lives when we give ourselves to Him."

And that's what it's all about in a nutshell: communicating the saving power of the gospel to kids most of society has given up on except to say, "Lock 'em up and throw away the key." But how? And who will do it?

CROSS-CULTURAL EDUCATION

Crossing the chasm from suburbia to city streets, from church sanctuary to jail chapel, is one way both church and community leaders come face to face with Louie and Sam and Martin, Trigger and Pucho and Fox, not just as "street gang members" but as real people. Sometimes I bring the suburban folks into the city; sometimes I take "the guys" out to a suburban church or youth group or businessmen's meeting to tell their stories. Occasionally, with the permission of the young men involved, we will invite a key visitor to a United Nations meeting—an editor or TV anchor or business person.

Why? Because we want the mainstream world to see the other side of juvenile delinquency; behind the tough exterior are kids with overwhelming needs; behind the violence are rivals reaching out for peace in spite of the odds. Because we want people to consider whether God is calling them to befriend kids who desperately need real friends and who can introduce them to the best Friend of all.

Those who volunteer get quite an education, and most find it a positive experience. It takes time, however, to know the ways and lifestyle of another culture, and a wise ministry person will give that learning process top priority. Cultural differences affect more than just clothing style and music tastes. For instance, "Give me a straight answer" is a good Anglo phrase but very uncomfortable to an Asian or Hispanic used to talking more indirectly. "Look me right in the eye" is a frequent demand of Anglo authority figures, but to many nationalities it is a sign of disrespect; they look down when being addressed. Our volunteers certainly do not agree with all they see and hear on the streets, but they need to understand what is accepted there in order to relate to the kids.

What We Do and Why We Do It

Even though we make every effort to understand the cultural milieu in which these young gang members are nurtured, we are *not* a street ministry working directly with gangs. My staff of volunteers and I make most of our contacts at the youth section of the huge Cook County Jail or the Juvenile Detention Center. In both places we minister alongside the chaplains leading both group meetings and individual counseling sessions.

Wednesday mornings I spend with a unique group in a special section of the jail, young men in their late teens facing the most serious charges and having bail of $150,000 or more, or no bail at all. Many wait a year or more for their trials, so there is opportunity to get to know them well. It is not unusual to have fifty or more young men at this service, at which time we challenge them to make a Christian commitment and give them instruction in spiritual growth. Friday nights other volunteers join me for personal counseling sessions with more seekers than we have time to see, all eager to learn more of the Lord and His Word.

It is through these guys that we meet their gang buddies. We know most of these kids well before they are released, and we are accepted on the streets because *they* are the ones who take us there.

Out on the streets, we meet with the kids wherever they agree to meet: a park, a fast-food restaurant, a kid's basement, or a garage. We keep their confidence to the limit allowed by law and are available when they face a crisis. We talk with their parents and try to bring healing to broken and strained relationships. We sometimes testify in court when we believe in a boy and can be of help. Courtrooms are scary places to these youth, and, guilty or not guilty, they need a friend.

But there are things we will not do. We do not loan them money or bail them out of jail, though we will sign a juvenile out of custody and take him home. Rather than a loan, a staff person can give a boy some money if he or she can afford it; but debt obligations tend to destroy a relationship. The kids can freely help our program when they choose to, and they very often do; but any work they do for us personally must be for reasonable pay.

OVERCOMING THE BARRIERS . . . TAKES A MIRACLE

We try to find jobs for some of our young people, and we draw on a network of community resources to help. But that's easier said than done, for most of these kids have little or no job history, have never learned responsibility, and often lack transportation to areas away from their homes where the jobs are. Also, a kid cannot take a job if he has to go through enemy territory to get to it or if the workplace itself is in opposition turf. And frankly, some of them have trouble passing a drug test.

Employers who are willing to help these young men nonetheless demand consistent, good work—something our kids have little experience producing. Preparing them for a job interview, filling out applications, and knowing what is expected on the job is a major assignment fraught with frustration. We have also met a few employers—including church members, unfortunately—who take advantage of our kids, trying to pay less than the minimum wage and giving them cash instead of a check to avoid taxes and social security requirements.

Getting them into school is not much easier. Urban schools are quick to dump kids who have been a problem as fast as the law allows, and getting a school outside their district to take them is another excruciating challenge, and the kids do not help their own cause. Most of them do not seem to know that school runs five days a week, and it comes as a real shock when they learn they are expected to come on time and stay for the full day.

Most of these kids sleep till late afternoon and get up asking the most important question for the day: "Where is the party tonight?" They turn up the TV, slap a movie in the VCR, switch on the radio (all at full blast), or get high on drugs—anything to act as an anesthetic to deaden the pain of an empty life. Breaking that cycle involves a real commitment from a street kid and the patience of Job from our staff.

In the institutions and on the streets we meet workers from other church and community programs and are grateful for them. Youth For Christ's urban ministry teams are reaching out in many communities; while in Los Angeles I came to respect the efforts of World Opportunities, as well as the services of people such as Dr. Keith Phillips, Rozie Grier, and Dr. E. V. Hill. David Wilkerson, famed author of *The Cross and the Switchblade*, has returned to New York City to pastor Times Square Church with a unique outreach to the street kids in the area. In Chicago we rub shoulders with good people from the Crisis Intervention Network and Youth at Risk, as well as the dedicated ministry staff of Inner-City Impact, the Friends Youth Center at Cabrini Green, and Jesus People USA, all faithfully serving on the front line of need. I serve the community in a different area as a member of the Illinois Juvenile Justice Commission, a concerned group of professionals and citizens appointed by the governor to help state government deal with the enormous challenges presented by at-risk young people.

DEALING WITH ATTITUDES AND VALUES

In meeting with street kids we constantly deal with their feelings toward enemies and contrast their attitudes with Jesus' responses. The apostle Paul wrote, "If your enemy is hungry, feed him; if he is thirsty, give him something to drink" (Romans 12:20).

"Does that mean I gotta buy one of *those* guys a Big Mac® and a Coke®?" a kid will ask incredulously. They are amazed to learn that the Bible is very straightforward about what it says.

Our task as "ambassadors for Christ" is to bring a message of reconciliation, both in their relationship to God and with each other (2 Corinthians 5:19-20). Their challenge is to be part of the answer on troubled streets instead of being part of the problem.

Facing the truth is not pleasant for any of us, and my young congregation is no exception. They are quick to find an easy way out, shift the blame to others, or evade the issue of their sins: "I got in with the wrong crowd" . . . "I was in the wrong place at the wrong time" . . . "It wasn't really my fault, I just. . . ." I used to get angry when I thought kids were lying to me; now I respond more with sadness, because long before a kid lies to me, he has lied to himself, and there are no lies any of us believe faster than the ones we tell ourselves.

But the young men who come to our services are looking for assurance and forgiveness and want the genuine love only the Lord can give. Repentance is a word we spend a good deal of time discussing, going beyond a sense of sorrow or regret to turning away from a lifestyle and habits that are wrong and destructive, as well as offensive to God.

The crimes some of these young offenders have committed are more than mistakes; we are dealing with sins against a Holy God (Psalm 51:4). Changes in evil and selfish lifestyles do not always come easily or quickly, but they *will* come in a life genuinely turned over to Jesus and growing in friendship with Him (Philippians 1:6).

Not that any of us find it easy to relate to those who have committed horrible crimes or have attitudes we find repugnant. Except that Jesus spent much of His time with people just like that—undesirable, irreligious, morally sick. That is because He places value on the person. His love is not deterred by resistance, lust, money, power, and all the other lures of Satan. Nor is it conditional. "I'll love you if . . ." or "I love you, but . . ." never fell from His lips but simply "I forgive you; go and sin no more."

God loves all of us, no matter what, and He wants us to be changed to be like Him. A love like that is beyond our natural inclinations, but when we begin to grasp it, we will throw away the labels and value each person—no matter what.

A Mission Field for the Church

For the young men who leave the county jail or juvenile detention center to serve time in prison, we rely on the state chaplains and volunteers from Prison Fellowship, Bill Glass Ministries, and other programs to build on the spiritual foundation we have laid. I encourage church and community leaders to support those programs and others like them, including Chaplain Ray who distributes thousands of Bibles and helpful books to prisoners everywhere.

But our primary goal is to relate these young people to a local church, and that is one of our hardest tasks. First of all, many churches with facilities, staff, and resources to serve young people have left the inner city and relocated in the suburbs. Of course, there are many churches still in the city, and some have been adopted as sister congregations by their suburban counterparts. A few of these are reaching out in their community to serve in solid, consistent, and unheralded ways.

For instance, Lawndale Community Church on Chicago's troubled West Side supplements its weekly worship with schools, medical clinics, food pantries, family counseling, and recreation. LaSalle Street Church pioneered a legal clinic for Cabrini area residents who need help with civil and criminal court cases, one of the few instances in which the Christian legal profession has been brought into criminal defense work, where they are desperately needed. But there are still great shortages in meeting the needs of inner-city youth. Few churches in the most deprived areas have a youth program or a staff to lead it.

Second, some churches frankly do not want us bringing our gang kids, converted or not, into their services. As a pastor told one of our volunteers asking to use his church for one of our gatherings and also anxious to bring the kids to Sunday services, "Keep those kids away from here. What would my deacons say if one of their daughters told her dad she was going out with a gang member she met at our youth group? I won't hear of it!" And that ended that.

Third, other churches are caught up in tangents and excesses that make it difficult for us to look to them as a spiritual resource for our kids. A few extremists equate feistiness with faithfulness, preaching a long list of what they are against and not much that's positive; others confuse an emotional high with spiritual depth and suffer a real letdown when confronted with the realities of life; then there are the "wanabees" of the church world, who think economic and social rehabilitation can substitute for spiritual rebirth. All these groupings abound in the city.

Fourth, we often cannot get a street kid to attend church if it is in the wrong territory. Crossing enemy lines for worship may get him to heaven faster than God intended. And not all the kids' motives are the best. Three members of the Insane Popes planned a hit on a rival, knowing that it was the victim's custom to attend church each Sunday evening. What could be easier than to find him in the church parking lot after services and finish him off? But when they arrived at the church, they wondered, "How do we know he's even here tonight?" They decided to go in and find out.

As they stood at the back looking over the congregation the pastor leading the service suddenly greeted them from the pulpit. "I see we have three young brothers from the area who have come to visit us. Don't be hesitant, gentlemen, come right in. Ushers, show them up here to these fine seats at the front!" Not knowing how to respond they hastily shoved their weapons further into their jacket pockets and followed the cheerful usher up through the congregation. Much later they told me about the incident and added, "We actually liked the service!" The boy they were seeking was not there.

We need more churches that are willing to open their doors, develop effective youth programs, and fund staff to meet the needs of inner-city youth. Because if we don't, the vacuum will be filled by others.

The "isms" and cults are making significant inroads among disadvantaged urban youth, none stronger than the appeal of the Black Muslims, who have adapted the Muslim message to the contemporary American scene.[3] Their inroads

3. An insightful look at the Muslim movement, its belief system, and its impact on our society is provided by Phil Parshall in *The Cross and the Crescent* (Wheaton, Ill.: Tyndale, 1989).

among young black inmates at correctional facilities have been enormous, primarily because they are addressing crucial issues too often ignored by Christians, such as poverty, drugs, racism, and injustice. And they proclaim action-oriented solutions.

But these competing religious voices offer either the wrong savior or no savior at all. It is here that Christianity and Jesus have an exclusive invitation: "Salvation is found in no one else" (Acts 4:12), and Jesus' bold pronouncement "I am the way and the truth and the life. No one comes to the Father except through me" (John 14:6). All those who settle for Jesus as a great teacher or another prophet or even God's greatest creation are classified as "a thief and a robber" (John 10:1), trying to get through the gate some other way.

It is the certainty and authority of salvation through Christ, and the positive impact transformed people can have on their world, that should compel us to reach out to the mission field that is just around the corner in our own cities and suburbs.

THE DIFFERENCE VOLUNTEERS MAKE

Jesus works through His people, not all of them professional youth workers by any means! Jesus calls His people "salt" (Matthew 5:13), and salt does not make a difference sitting on a shelf or in the shaker. But it really has an impact when it's tossed into the middle of things and stirred up.

A busy suburban homemaker gives one evening a week to counsel with young girls at the Juvenile Detention Center and finds it one of the most important experiences in her life. A professional man takes an evening to spend time with some young gang members and has become almost a second father to the group. One store owner, too busy to take on a regular group activity, acts as a mentor to one inner-city boy; he sees him regularly and phones him frequently. During the summer break from school, he plans on bringing the boy into his store to teach him about the business.

Not all of the kids we work with in our institutional programs make it once they are back on the streets, and it's easy to say they were not sincere. That is possible; but most often the follow-up support needed in the Christian community was not there in the face of the strong lures and temptations of the streets. Besides a good church home, one of the most critical needs is for a caring friend—pastor, youth leader, youthful peer, caring adult—to take a personal interest in each youth. Here is a tremendous challenge from the one who said, "Whatever you did for one of the least of these brothers of mine, you did for me" (Matthew 25:40).

To be a volunteer working with urban youth is to dare to be involved with sinners without being involved in their sin. Few assignments require greater need of the weapons of spiritual warfare that provide protection—truth, righteousness, readiness, faith, and salvation (Ephesians 6:11-18).

Some imagine dealing with juvenile offenders to be exciting and glamorous, a way to relieve the monotony and boredom of their own lives. Others are too forceful and do not take the time to be a friend and earn the right to be heard. Some discourage easily when there is not an immediate response. Others fear personal danger on the streets, though the kids are very protective of our volunteers. College students are often idealistic in their desire to transform a whole gang or neighborhood but are not usually available long enough to build up credibility in the community.

There are other less tangible but very real concerns. The majority of our institutional population is African-American and Hispanic with a few whites and a growing number of Asians. Ideally minorities are most effective in ministering to their own people, though there is certainly no reason to avoid cross-racial contacts. Many successful minority people have moved away from the troubled streets to the suburbs and have no desire to return to the old neighborhoods, even for ministry. Other volunteers are quite adept at activities with young people—sports, mechanics, camping, and so forth—but have little or no experience at relating the gospel message and giving the spiritual guidance that is the foundation of our ministry. Of course, there are exceptions to all these limitations, but those are the general concerns we must address in enlisting help for our work.

But in spite of these challenges, we need all sorts of men and women who can give a "tithe" of their time to work with these kids. That is something many people rarely imagine themselves doing. Yet by using common sense, a volunteer is actually very safe in the neighborhoods. We go into an area only to see young people we know; we are their friends and are introduced as such in their circle. Under such conditions a volunteer is quite safe. (I keep reminding the suburbanites that the most dangerous part of the evening is the drive into town on the expressway avoiding drunk drivers.)

Tom Locke of Moody Bible Institute, a young black man who grew up in Cleveland, added much to our staff, especially in his ability to minister to African-American young people. He started with us as part of his ministry training and was instrumental in adding other students seeking on-the-field ministry experience. He also opened up the excellent resources at the school's Life Sciences-Urban Ministry Center for our unique ministry project.

Tom sees both the joy of urban ministry and the heartbreak. "It's sad to see the consequences of kids' choices. 'Be sure your sins will find you out' plays out in the physical, mental, and spiritual areas of broken lives," Tom observes. But he is also there when kids turn to the Lord and begin the process of growing in the faith and growing away from the gang-infection and habits that destroy so many.

Inside the institutions or on the street, other staff leaders and I work alongside volunteers, having them watch us, then doing it with us, then having us watch as they develop their own ministry role and expertise. It's the Timothy principle in action: "The things you have heard me say in the presence of many witnesses entrust to reliable men who will also be qualified to teach others" (2 Timothy 2:2).

But What Can I Do?

Put on the volunteer's hat for a moment. What could you do?

First, get personally involved in the local jails by leading Bible studies, counseling with kids, listening, assisting with chaplain services, and visiting youthful offenders waiting long months for their case to come up.

Second, a caring adult can be a friend to a street youth. Take him to a ball game, go on a camping trip, invite him to church, meet with his buddies at MacDonalds or Burger King for an informal talk about the kids' lives and how the Word of God can guide them through tough places.

Third, pray for kids by name.

Fourth, give money and resources to support programs that are helping kids in the prisons or on the streets.

Fifth, help your suburban church link up with an inner-city church that is trying to minister to its community. Support them with your prayers, finances, and volunteer help.

Sixth, reach out to victims. Has a young person been murdered in your area, a family robbed? The pain of these losses lasts for a long time. There may already be a group in your area through which you might volunteer (e.g., Parents of Murdered Children; Compassion). Encourage restitution for victims, or simply be willing to visit the homes and families of those touched by violence.

Seventh, be a voice of intelligent concern about what is happening to our youth today. Write letters, vote wisely, attend community and school meetings dealing with drugs, gang activity, drop-out or push-out problems, charges of police brutality, activities for youth.

Many volunteers tell me they will not give a kid their home address or phone number. I never argue, but after a while they usually end up bringing their key youths home to meet the family and have a good time together. We have *never* had one such family contact abused or the confidence misplaced. Treat kids with kindness and respect, even tough street kids, and they will almost always return it. Conversely, tell a kid he's no good and rotten long enough and he may go out and prove his critics right. Kids have an amazing way of living up to our expectations.

Leading a Bible study at a juvenile institution, assisting at chapel services, giving personal counseling, making street visits, or supervising activities are all ways caring men and women can share God's love with hurting kids. And most of those who have stepped out of their comfortable routines into the lives of these kids say it is one of the most rewarding experiences of their Christian life.

It is love that makes a difference.

HEADIN' HOME

My suburban visitors to Cook County Jail noticed that Lord Zapp had sat quietly throughout the session, so one of them asked if he would like to tell his experience.

I encouraged him to respond, and he did. That Zapp ended up at age seventeen in jail on a serious charge was not surprising—it was inevitable.

Shortly before he was born in Chicago, his father, a military veteran, went to prison for killing the man who raped Zapp's sister. Later, after his dad was paroled home and Zapp was eleven years old, his two brothers were shot and killed on the street. The anger and hostility in young Zapp was like a raging inferno. Though he was young and small, he was determined to take his brothers' position on the streets in the Vice Lord organization.

The streets became his world, the big dope dealers with the fancy cars his heroes, and the pretty young ladies his conquests—he fathered four children out of wedlock by age seventeen. It was a life of thrills and action, with money that came and went easily. But there is a downside to that fast life, and for Zapp it was his arrest on robbery and murder charges.

"I brought my rank from the streets to jail," Zapp explained to his attentive listeners, "and I didn't see no need to change things, nor was there a chance if I wanted to."

Still he was restless. It was not only his pending trial that bothered him; the challenge came from within. "I wasn't meant to live this way, to hurt, hate, and destroy. People aren't there just so I can use them to make money and settle personal scores. But where do I start to turn around?"

To his credit he went looking. There were several other Christian guys on his jail tier, including his own cellmate, the Professor from the Latin Brothers, who probably influenced Zapp at a time when no one else could.

"The Professor got me seriously into the Bible. That's great stuff to read," Zapp explained. "But I didn't just need *something*—I had tried lots of somethings only to be disappointed or fall back into the old rut. But when I asked Jesus to call the shots in my life, some very good things started happening, and they still are."

Lord Zapp joined his cellmate in seeking to help other young men on their deck, including opposition members from the streets.

"I'm sorry it took coming to jail to bring me to the Lord," he concluded, "but better this way than not at all."

A bell rang announcing the end of evening activities. Our young men would have to return to their cell-block. My civilian guests lingered, trying to grasp all they had heard in the past two hours. Several told me they were going back to tell their friends at church about the jail and the mission field it represents.

"This has been an amazing experience," said one, walking out with tearful eyes.

But will they return? Will you be with them? I hope so.

Afterword

The ministry to troubled youth described on these pages has been developed with the help of many friends through the years, including volunteers and generous people whose support and encouragement made a most significant contribution. Among them are Dorothy Norman, Paul Yearout, Dr. Herb Tyler, Dr. Frank Phillips, Dr. Roy McKeown, Dr. Robert A. Cook, Dr. Ted W. Engstrom, Jack and Mary Jean Hamilton, Paul and Nancy Stolz, Stan and Anita Johnson, Gilmore and Dresden Erickson, Dr. Jay Kesler, Ed Rose, Franklin Robbie, Bufford Karraker, Jack Daniel, and Bob Simpson.

The ministry in Chicago was begun with the encouragement of Bruce Love and William Fields and built on an excellent foundation of community respect developed by Shirley Holloway, Tom Lach, and David Parker, all of whom are now in church ministries. Our Youth For Christ institutional services are under the sponsorship of Good News Mission in Chicago and their chaplains, Rick Gawenda, Harry Roundtree, and Steve Thompson. In area Illinois youth correctional facilities we ministered in cooperation with former Chaplain Melvin Perkins and Father Jack Heraty. A most helpful friend to the ministry is John F. Browne, chief juvenile probation officer of Cook County, along with national officials, especially Judge Bertil E. Johnson of Tacoma, Washington, and Richard Bothman, Leonard Raimirez, and Charles Alexander from the juvenile probation department in San José, California.

I am especially grateful to my home churches for their prayers and support when I served in their community: Central Baptist Church, Tacoma, Washington; Los Gatos Christian Church, Los Gatos, California; and now Christ Church of Oak Brook, Illinois, and its founding pastor, Dr. Arthur H. DeKruyter.

In preparing this book I note with special thanks the generous help and encouragement of some young people who provided excellent material: Curtis Croft, Mario Flores, Demetrius Henderson, Mike Herman, Levy Jackson, Joel Mayoral, "Burn" Mendia, José Quinones, Frank Robinson, and Tony Snelius, along with many Chicago street youth and correctional center residents who generously offered their assistance and experiences for these pages. The stories of various young people are true, though some nonessential details were altered to protect confidentiality.

Background on juvenile and institutional issues was provided by material from the National Council on Crime and Delinquency, the Illinois Juvenile Justice Commission, and the excellent reports of Glenn Emery in *Insight* magazine.

Informational Resources

Readers desiring additional reading material are referred to these among the many excellent books available:

Criminal Violence, Criminal Justice, by Charles Silberman (Random House), a comprehensive overview of the American justice system. A unique perspective on inner-city youth problems is well written by Carl Taylor in *Dangerous Society* (Michigan State U. Press). *Inside the Criminal Mind,* by Stanton E. Samenow (Random House), offers the best analysis ever published on the thinking of the criminal offender and how best to deal with it. *Convicted,* by Charles Colson and Daniel Van Ness (Crossway), presents a concise biblical perspective on criminal justice issues. Another Colson book, *Against the Night* (Vine), probes the attitudes and mores of our day that challenge the basics of our spiritual beliefs in this country. A colleague of Colson, Van Ness also describes a practical, biblical approach to crime, punishment, and restitution in *Crime and Its Victims*

(InterVarsity). The same publisher also released a discussion guide by Mr. Colson titled *Justice.*

Anthony Evans provides an insightful challenge to the church to face the urban crisis in *America's Only Hope* (Moody). *Justice and Mercy*, by Donald Smarto (Tyndale), gives a Christian solution to America's correctional crisis. Smarto also wrote *Pursued* (InterVarsity), a highly recommended book of personal experience and ministry service.

Whatever Became of Sin? (Hawthorn) and *The Crime of Punishment* (Viking), by the late Dr. Karl Menninger, are classics in the field of attitudes toward deviant behavior and those who commit it.

An unusual and compelling look at the criminal justice system through the experiences of a prosecutor is given in *Rough Justice* (Pantheon), and some good insights to the problems of drug enforcement are described in *Undercover*, by Donald Goddard (Dell), the true story of veteran federal agent Michael Levine. Also worthwhile are *At a Tender Age: Violent Youth and Juvenile Justice*, by Rita Kramer (Henry Holt), and *The Death Penalty for Juveniles*, by Victor Streib (Indiana U. Press).

Chief of Police Reuben Greenberg of Charleston, South Carolina, presents a compelling case for firm law enforcement in *Let's Take Back Our Streets* (Contemporary Books). A Loyola University, Chicago, assistant professor of journalism, Connie Fletcher, provides unique insight into the life and thinking of police in *What Cops Know* (Villard). I also recommend *[In]Justice for Juveniles*, by Ira M. Schwartz (Lexington). The book offers exciting new insights regarding juvenile crime control policies throughout the country.

Wyled Gates is an unlikely murder suspect—vice president of his high school class in East Chatham, New York, and logical choice for "most likely to succeed." But the seventeen year old was arrested and subsequently confessed to the brutal murder of four members of his family. Considering the confession suspect, jurors acquitted Gates, as well as a youth charged with supplying the murder weapon. Reporter Alan Gelb takes a critical look at how the justice system functioned in this instance in *Most Likely to Succeed* (Dutton).

Sociologist Terry Williams went out on New York streets to meet and spend time with members of a teenage dope-selling ring. The result is some unique insights in a book titled *The Cocaine Kids* (Addison-Wesley). Author Alex Kotlowitz vividly describes the problems of two Chicago brothers growing up in a housing project in *Are There No Children Here?* (Doubleday), whereas Thomas Weyr looks at the impact of the exploding Latino population in *Hispanics USA* (Harper & Row).

Most judges—male, white, and middle-class—have little understanding of racism or its influence on their thinking and conduct, writes Judge Bruce Wright. A New York Supreme Court justice, Wright draws on his experience as a black lawyer and a judge to talk about police power and the shortcomings of the justice system in *Black Robes, White Justice* (Lyle Stuart). Another view of the New York criminal justice system and its tragic effects in the life of one young man, Edmund Perry, is told in *Best Intentions*, by Robert Sam Anson (Random House).

In *Dr. Dobson Answers Your Questions* (Tyndale), the president of Focus on the Family presents practical answers to the questions parents and youth counselors are seeking. Three other helpful books are *When Caring Parents Have Problem Kids*, by Finley Sizemore, (Revell); *Why Good Parents Have Bad Kids*, by E. Kent Hayes (Doubleday); and *Ten Mistakes Parents Make with Teenagers (And How to Avoid Them)*, by Jay Kesler (Wolgemuth & Hyatt).

PROGRAM RESOURCES

A list of institutional ministries across the country is available from the Institute for Prison Ministry, Wheaton College, Wheaton, Illinois 60187. Phone: 708/752-5727.

A manual for beginning an institutional ministry and follow-up program for young offenders is available from Juvenile Institutional Ministry Network, Youth For Christ USA, Box 228822, Denver, Colorado 80222-8822.

Readers desiring to contact the Juvenile Justice Ministry may write to Metro Chicago Youth For Christ, 300 West Washington Street, Suite 416, Chicago, Illinois 60606. Phone: 312/443-1YFC. Richard Norton is executive director.

Finally, my grateful thanks to Dave and Neta Jackson, who brought their fine writing and editorial skills to this book, making it the interesting and positive contribution we want it to be in going behind the scenes to meet the troubled kids in the Cities of Lonesome Fear.

GORDON McLEAN